HALF MY SIZE WITH THE

Ridiculously

BIG

Salad

AMANDA ROSE, PH.D.

contents

Foreword

This book would not exist without the thousands of members of the Eat Like a Bear! community, their successes and struggles, and their ongoing interest in what I did during my year of dramatic weight loss. Through them I have come to understand far better what I did to lose the weight and what I need to keep doing to maintain my weight loss. I dedicate this book to them.

As members have adapted my framework to meet their own goals and lifestyles, we have learned a lot about weight-loss success factors. It is my hope that you too can find the pieces of the framework that will help you meet your own goals. In doing so, work with your doctor to adapt this framework to meet your unique needs and goals as, of course, you should always do before undertaking any new health regimen.

My Ph.D. is in the social sciences. I cannot write you a prescription or cast your broken arm. I am not that kind of doctor. Do not use this book as a doctor-replacement. It is simply based on my own personal experience with weight loss, which has come to impact thousands of people in a rather surprising fashion.

If you have found this book elsewhere, consider joining the Eat Like a Bear! community and digging in. The community is growing and evolving as we learn more about what specifically drives our success. To be sure, the Ridiculously Big Salad (RBS) is a monument to the food portion of our success, but we have a growing amount of content on what the community is calling the "Cooked RBS." In addition, I find myself spending an increasing amount of time on psychological success factors, rooted in my social science training in the psychology of choice, training that shaped the head game I played while losing 140 pounds, negotiating with that "devil on my shoulder," one micro-decision at a time. Do be sure to find us. It's anybody's guess what we'll be up to.

Amanda Rose
Spring 2020

Prologue

Way back, three years ago, when I was young and naive and I thought weight-loss diets were a bunch of baloney as I was laid up on my couch, desperately wanting to hike with my sons when I could only just limp across my house, I scheduled an appointment with a bariatric surgeon and began the process to be approved for bariatric surgery, a surgery I would never have and for which I no longer qualify.

I was the surgeon's ideal patient — I knew food, and I knew how to diet. I had the discipline to succeed, but I had not found the formula for losing weight. When I visited the surgeon in March 2017, I weighed in at 280 pounds (127 kg) of body weight and at 4,792 tons of desperation. The surgeon projected that I could reach 180 pounds (82 kg) with his gastric sleeve procedure, a loss of 100 pounds (45 kg), a weight at which I could walk across my house or even hike with my sons. In those dark, desperate days, I envisioned my future at 180 pounds. I would walk without limping. I was ready.

When I showed up at the surgeon's office nearly two years later at 140 pounds (64 kg), having lost 40 percent more weight than he had projected, all on my own, the surgeon's staff was astounded. Apparently not many patients of bariatric surgeons return two years later, half their size. In fact, in the final meeting I had with the nutritionist for the bariatric surgery, before all of my weight loss, I asked that if I risked losing so much weight would I no longer qualify for the surgery. She looked directly into my eyes, shook her head left to right, and said, "No. As long as you have more than 40 percent body fat, you will qualify. You will not lose that much on your own." The words seem unsupportive now, but she spoke them with such heart that I left her office with a glimmer of hope for my future.

As it would turn out, my schedule and the surgeon's did not align for some months. My desperation was thereby channeled in an unexpected way, the basis of this book. I got started and somehow lost not only 40 percent more weight than promised with that bariatric surgery, but I also saved thousands of dollars in doing so. I ate more calories in the process, and my lifelong calorie and nutrition intake will be much higher. As a happy addition (as I flagrantly show in a video on YouTube), I do not have the skin sag that plagues bariatric patients, sometimes requiring tens of thousands of dollars in additional surgery and the accompanying surgery risk.

Those facts are mind-blowing in themselves, but the story really gets far better. In the spring of 2018, my friends and family started asking what I was doing and adopted my approach. My blood relatives who have struggled with weight have a pretty impressive success rate in implementing my way of eating: 100 percent. Each of us is now slimmer than we have been since we were thirty years old. About half of us are slimmer than we have ever been as adults. Frankly, as a family of fatties, we are pretty pleased with ourselves.

In the spring of 2018, a couple of ladies found me on Facebook and implemented my approach with success. They inspired me to start a little Facebook group called Eat Like a Bear!, a reference to a video I created on Facebook in the spring of 2018, a bit tongue-in-cheek, with no mindfulness of what was brewing at the time, a story I tell at the end of this book. The Eat Like a Bear! community began to grow, and I still did not appreciate that we had a very distinct and replicable approach to weight loss. I was hesitant in those early days to give people a specific framework of eating because I feel strongly that we each need to find our own way with food and that a culture of food diversity is a winning strategy for any community. However, as the community grew, more people said to me: "*I want to know exactly what you ate.*"

In January 2019, Nancy nudged me further with this post to our Eat Like a Bear! community:

"*Amanda Rose is the Mama Bear. She lost 140 lbs doing one meal a day and intermittent fasting. . . . She says to keep it simple. A giant salad, good fat, and a protein. The very inspirational and motivational speaker Tony Robbins said in some of his material to find someone who has been successful and mimic them. I highly recommend leaning on her testimony.*"

Nancy had been in the community long enough to notice my "giant salad," and I began to realize that the salad model was the most effective meal type for group members. It also happened that I ate salads about four out of five days during my period of intensive weight loss. I felt more urgency to communicate my "salad-eating," and I began to show my actual salads in live videos on Facebook. Community members started making their own salads, and our success rates seemed to improve. I got more requests for a salad recipe book, a request I thought at first was ludicrous because who *really* needs a salad recipe? I was busy and over-whelmed by life at that moment but decided to set aside *an entire week* to write a salad e-book. I planned to beg or buy help from friends and get it done. For some reason instead, I started the process on my own, alone in my kitchen, replicating the experience of my most intensive period of weight loss, an eight-month period in which I lost 100 pounds.

That "one-week recipe project" turned into months as I deconstructed my salads, painstakingly recording recipes and the nutrient profiles of each. By about the third week, I doubled down on the project and outsourced none of the work as I started to realize that this was not just a collection of salad recipes. I began to discover that what I ate all those months followed a distinct and highly replicable model, with elements that we probably should not dismiss or take for granted, especially as people implement variations of this concept with a little less success.

As I started on *The Ridiculously Big Salad* book and actually worked on measuring ingredients and being more systematic and intentional with the recipes, I whipped up Ridiculously Big Salads in my own kitchen and measured what was in them. I told people that I ate 1,000 to 1,200 calories in my salads, but the truth is that I measured very seldom. I measured a few of the salads way back in the fall of 2017, and then I just stopped bothering. I got into a groove that worked, and I never looked back. As I worked on this book and began to measure once again, it was a painstaking chore for my non-recipe-measuring self, but it awoke the social scientist in me and my time working on my Ph.D., and the whole process actually blew me away.

In the process of measuring, I discovered something fascinating: my dressing recipes, in the quantities I actually ate on the Ridiculously Big Salad each day over those eight months, fell in the 450 to 550 calorie range. One was below the range at 300 calories, and one was above it at

900 calories. The high-calorie exception was the dressing for the cheese-burger salad, and it was an eye-opener for me. The dressing contained nearly two times the calories because I used all mayonnaise instead of half mayonnaise and half Greek yogurt. I immediately adapted the dressing, adding the plain Greek yogurt in place of half the mayonnaise.

I am sure that those extra calories in that one salad dressing did not make a big difference in my progress, but you can imagine if all of my dressings followed the "mayonnaise only" blueprint over all those months — I would not have made nearly the same amount of progress that I did. That dressing would have added about 450 calories to my daily meals, and I would have lost about 4 pounds (2 kg) fewer each month, losing probably about 65 pounds (30 kg) in eight months instead of the 100 pounds (45 kg) I managed to lose.

All those many months, my subconscious was creating salad dressings that fit a framework. In fact, the whole salad had a framework, and the framework was critical to my success.

Make no mistake: the Ridiculously Big Salad *is* the reason I was able to capture these mind-blowing photos, one year apart, at the 45th parallel sign just north of Yellowstone National Park. This book is about the Ridiculously Big Salad, and I will show you how to build it for yourself, but first allow me to engage your mind in an important question: *Where will you be in one year?*

"A POSTCARD FROM YELLOWSTONE"

"Life can change completely in one year," I claim in a video I posted on Facebook in September 2018, "A Postcard from Yellowstone." The video brought many people to the Eat Like a Bear! Facebook group, most of whom were women as desperate as I was in the 2017 version of the Yellowstone photo. Some of their stories appear in this book. You can find many more stories on the internet. Before I introduce the stories, I will add that I do not believe that any of our photos or stories are anything exceptional. If you think we have something that you do not, some deep character trait that enabled us to succeed where you will fail, and if you happen to be a human reading this now, you are simply wrong. Let me explain.

In "A Postcard from Yellowstone," I discuss the hopelessness we feel as older, lifelong dieters, having tried diets over the years that only half-work and that are unsustainable. Have you ever considered what our experience in perpetual dieting failure does to our self-confidence? It is a formula for hopelessness, an experience with which far too many of us can relate.

Think about the preschooler who is given the little toy tool set that has a round peg, a triangular peg, and a square peg. She has a hammer, and she hammers the different pegs into the various holes of different shapes, learning her shapes by trial and error. While we might look at her little carpentry set and think she is just learning her shapes, she is also learning cause and effect, and, more importantly, she learns that she can impact the world with her actions. She is learning self-confidence with a little wooden hammer and a set of geometric pegs, right there on a rug in preschool. As she grows up and tries to influence her world with her choices and actions, what does she learn with her first dieting failure? How about her second?

Low fat? Vegan? Atkins? Hammer. Hammer. Hammer.

High fat? Macrobiotic? Medifast? Hammer. Hammer. Hammer.

South Beach? Cabbage soup? Grapefruit? Hammer. Hammer. Hammer.

Weight Watchers? SlimFast? Coconut oil? Hammer. Hammer. Hammer.

What if we were locked into some sort of hellish, fiery, Sisyphean preschool with that carpentry tool, with no peg that quite fit, hammering away, wearing our ineptitude around preschool like a giant fat suit? If the preschool carpentry set teaches us self-confidence, what are we taught in that fiery pit?

We have lived for decades watching our self-confidence erode under society's judgment of our fat bodies and under our own inability to effect change in our physical selves. As our confidence erodes and our hopelessness creeps in, we are perceived to be out of control, weak, fat, and lazy. Do not underestimate the seriousness of this situation: In mental health research, hopelessness is a strong predictor of suicide. We have lived for years hammering away, increasingly desperate for change and increasingly hopeless that we have any control at all. The judgment from others we feel increases. We get fatter. We feel weak and out of control because, in fact, everyone around us thinks we are.

Sure, the food we are eating or the alcohol we are drinking contributes to our ever-enlarging fat suit. Why do we make such bad decisions deep down in that fiery pit? Let us think about the psychology of our decisions from the point of view of someone who has always been fat. I might look at a cocktail, as I sit there fat, and recognize intellectually that I could guzzle the cocktail and gain a half pound of fat overnight. Do I drink it? If I do not drink the cocktail, I am fat. If I drink the cocktail, I am fatter. I sit in a fiery pit looking at something that will bring me immediate comfort, be it a cocktail, a bag of chips, a cookie, or all of the above, and my choice set is *"fat or fatter?"* What do I decide to do? Do I drink the cocktail? As a person with extensive field research on this particular topic, the answer is so obvious that I do not consider it to be a real question.

When the choice set is *"trim or fat?,"* your whole calculus changes, a change I can only report from here on the other side, a choice I found unexpectedly at the age of forty-nine. Cocktails are excessive, life-sucking contrivances when your actual choice set is *"trim or fat?"*

Absolutely, our actions matter, but when we are stuck in a pit of despair and hopelessness, the psychology of our choices is warped by the lack of tools available to us and by the pain of our own experience.

When we are limping around or immobile due to knee and hip injuries, when we have feet so swollen from congestive heart failure that they do not even look like feet, or when we have nerve pain from diabetic neuropathy and fear losing our limbs, hopelessness can take deep root in our souls, especially if we have learned over many decades that weight-loss diets do not work. We find ourselves laid up and fat, desperate for any lifeline at all, but all too often too hopeless to find the lifeline. The fact that we can even live to this point of desperation is a testament to our strength, not our weakness.

If any of this story resonates with you at all, you are actually stronger than you think you are. We are survivors of a painful life experience and act from an instinct to survive, not from weakness, lack of discipline, or inherent laziness. Your strength is there even if your path out is clouded by pain and despair.

The focus and strength I see every day in the Eat Like a Bear! community is the stuff of primal survival, an actual biological urge to live, not any special character trait. Biology drives us to apply the discipline to save ourselves, once we set aside the lifelong message that we cannot control our own weight and that dieting does not work.

After decades of learning that we have little control over our weight, I do not expect you to unlearn that message with any words I write in this book. My goal is for you to *set the message aside* long enough to test the method I describe. I have a peg right here, and it continues to amaze me how many of us have been missing it all these years.

Every single day in our community I see people picking up that hammer and pounding on that peg like conditioned Olympic athletes and changing their lives completely, launching themselves right out of that fiery pit. It is the stuff of primal survival, and it is powerful.

I say often that the oxygen of our community is our desperation, and it should not be a surprise that the Eat Like a Bear! community stands out in its ability to lose a whole lot of weight. I have lost far more than I ever imagined possible, and the reason is partly trite — the diet works — but I am going to tell you a story anyway, because I get a lot of comments from naysayers that my success is fueled by some superhuman character trait that I happen to possess and that they do not. As I mentioned above, I expect that character plays a very small role in the story of our community.

We are losing a whole lot of weight, getting through the very long grind of weight loss like we have never been able to before, not because of our character but because we are simply fueled by our own success. It was the case with me, and I witness it daily in our community. There is always a life-changing moment of clarity, and mine was in November 2017. I had lost 20 pounds (9 kg) to be approved for bariatric surgery but had then lost nearly 50 pounds (23 kg) more by that November day. I was down to about 210 pounds (95 kg).

It was an autumn day, and the weather was changing here in my home in California's Giant Sequoia National Monument. I headed out for a walk on our mountain road, one that I have walked since 1982. The oak leaves were falling and rustling on the ground, and new winter grasses were starting to sprout, as they had for 35 years. I had not walked on the road for eleven months, due to a knee injury. Getting out in such a familiar place with its forest aromas was wonderfully comforting and familiar. It was delightful, and I probably should have been ready for what happened next, but I was taken by surprise. As I was taking it all in and basking in the total physical experience of walking in nature, about 200 yards (180 meters) in I came to a stop, and I stood there, looking and listening. I walked for another 30 yards (27 meters), and I slowed again, looking and listening. I stood there on that November day, at first almost perplexed because I had not considered what might happen out on that walk. The total physical experience of that walk was *completely different,* and it was not because the leaves were out of season, or because the vulture migration was six weeks behind, or because some wildfire left a scar on the land. The *difference was me,* and it blew my mind. The total physical experience of that November 2017 walk was completely different because *I was completely different.* I was "only" down 70 pounds (32 kg), but those 70 pounds changed my life. My entire physical experience was simply changed. That was the moment I knew that I would not be getting bariatric surgery, and it is the moment I consider to be the greatest success of my life.

I ask in "The Postcard from Yellowstone" how much life can change in one year, but the raw fact is that my life changed completely in three months, by November 2017, at 210 pounds (95 kg). I did not need to be a trimmer 140 pounds (63 kg), 30 pounds (14 kg) below my lowest adult weight, to be successful. Way back in November 2017, at 210 pounds, I won, right out there on that mountain road.

Why did I not stop there? People ask how I got through the long grind, and, it is true, I certainly could have stopped. Why did I not? *I had trained my entire life for that moment.* It simply never occurred to me to stop.

Why are members of the Eat Like a Bear! community apparently far more likely to grind their way down to their high school weights, at the ripe ages of fifty, sixty, seventy, and eighty? *We have trained our entire lives for this moment.*

TRANSFORM

There was something deeper happening as well in the fall of 2017. When you are beaten up and haggard over all of the decades, wielding that hammer and trying to maintain even a tiny sliver of self-confidence, grasping for every little bit of hope, and then your actions actually start to have an impact, your inside is transformed at least as much as your outside. I found myself more competent and bold every day. I could feel that internal power growing as those months passed.

In the Eat Like a Bear! community the tagline is *"No surgery, no drugs, no special branded products. Required: Your own bootstraps."* You might think that it is simply because I do not want to run around selling a bunch of junk that only half works, and that is certainly true. However, my core reason for the tagline is this: If you can launch yourself out of the fiery pit, *on your own strength*, then your internal transformation is likely to be far more powerful than what you can contemplate at this moment. Like a rock transformed by fire and pressure, you are metamorphosed. No pharmaceutical or supplement will ever be as effective as your own actions if you simply keep your head down and focus. Do not overlook the benefit of going without them. Let's not let drugs or branded diet accelerator products take from us the personal growth that awaits.

For me, this internal transformation is unexpected, and, as I have used the hammer and peg analogy with psychologists and describe my transformation, it makes perfect sense, but it took some real field research down in that fiery pit to report back on my findings to the mental health profession. When I get this far into the discussion, they have not asked, "How are you able to maintain your weight *this time*?" Back in the surgeon's office in 2017, maintaining my weight loss was my core concern, as it should have been. I still think about it every single day, as a discipline primarily, but I do not *worry* that I will be 280 pounds (127 kg) (or more) again. I am simply not the same person that I was in March 2017 when I sat in that bariatric surgeon's office. The process of losing 140 pounds (64 kg), of keeping my head down and grinding for months, not only instilled in me new habits but has also *transformed me completely*. This point is not lost on the psychologists.

Why does the Eat Like a Bear! community have some of the most powerful emerging weight-loss cases in the most unexpected demographic: older women? You simply cannot launch yourself out of the fiery pit without going through a powerful personal transformation. We have brand-new people emerging in our community, transformed by fire and pressure, metamorphosed, and, unexpectedly, ridiculously successful. I think about them as I write this book and blast my secret theme song (*which I whisper to you here: Queen's "Under Pressure"*). As I reflect on what is happening in our community, I am not surprised that it is our members who start in some of the deepest places in that fiery pit whom I see hammering their way to a new life, right past our members who have "only" a couple of pants sizes to lose. Extreme heat and pressure transform solid rock, and apparently people, too. The more intense the heat and the stronger the pressure, the more likely is the complete metamorphosis. You will find these members in the community watching for your arrival because they "get it" like no one else ever will.

LAUNCH

Nearly every day someone says to me, "*I am not you. I cannot do it.*" As I see it, if you look around yourself and see a pit of fire, you need nothing else to make this work. If you could teleport yourself to March 2017, I might look a lot like you do now. I am not the same "me" today as I was when I was down in that pit. Do not look at my confidence as the *cause* of my success. It is, rather, the result.

The strength that I mustered in those very early days to wield that hammer one more time came from desperation and the primal urge to survive. It is what I consider to be the oxygen of the Eat Like a Bear! community. Desperation is simply our biggest success factor. Once we get past the long-learned message that "No, we can't" and see that when it works, it works big, our biological drive to thrive kicks in, and the momentum builds. That is what happened to me in November 2017, and I see it every day in our community. Some of us take a step outside, sometimes for the first time in a very long time, and we take an actual walk out in the fresh air with our feet on the earth. We might even find ourselves barefoot out there, as our declining weight puts less pressure on every square centimeter of our haggard feet, allowing us to feel the earth between our toes without pain, walking, barefooted, for the first time in many years. Transformed. Barefooted. *BearFooted.*

THE COMMUNITY

Our community is filled with amazing stories, and I highlight just a few here, primarily to get you to seek out others.

Shelley joined the group on the very first day, July 9, 2018. She was also the first active and official member to lose 100 pounds (45 kg). Shelley helped forge the "bear" culture of the group, early on posting bear graphics and memes that were affirming and highly connected to the group members. Shelley was then tested a few months later by a major family crisis. She moved from rapid weight-loss mode to a maintenance phase. She made it through a stressful stint, in maintenance, until she was ready to focus more and lose more weight. By spring of 2019 she hit the "century-down" mark and celebrated with a 5K walk. She did so in the midst of ongoing family stresses, the type that hit most of us and that make the weight struggle even more difficult. She has lost more than 130 pounds (59 kg) as I write

this and is organizing community members to join her next spring for another 5K. She has not hit her maintenance weight (and, like many of us, may not even know what that weight is), but her life has changed completely. She is no longer prediabetic. She is off three blood pressure medications as well as medications for asthma and anxiety.

Maria found the group in January 2019 via the video "A Postcard from Yellowstone." She is well known in the group because she posted a weekly photo of her progress, each week displaying her "before" photo alongside her "progress" photo. Every single week, her photos popped out of the screen, increasingly filled with fire and charisma as her life changed. She is now down more than 120 pounds (54 kg) and in maintenance.

Maria's story is interesting because she studied my approach and structured a personalized plan, one more systematic than the one I implemented. In fact, I told her that her approach is very much what I might have done had I followed a specific model way back when. Her model is highly regimented, strict, and effective. Each week she implemented an extended water fast of seventy-two hours from Saturday afternoon until Tuesday. Tuesday through Friday she ate one meal a day, often a Ridiculously Big Salad, and Saturday she joined her husband for meals and ate a bit more, albeit always ketogenic food. In doing so, Maria hit the 100-pound (45 kg) loss mark in just seven months.

I was able to meet Maria in person, and what struck me in speaking to her was that she had formed a strong habit of that weekly seventy-two-hour fast. Even entering maintenance, she planned to continue it because it had simply become a part of her life. It was that discussion with Maria that made me appreciate the power of habit in a deeper way. I actually felt a bit jealous that I had not mindfully crafted such a specific structure for myself.

Of the many other people in the community, I would be remiss not to mention those who are especially dear to my heart because of their progress with Type 2 diabetes. I write to you from California's diabetes and obesity capital. My own great grandmother and great uncle both died as double amputees due to complications from diabetes.

Two of the moms from my local school community are early adopters in the Eat Like a Bear! community. In fact, Anna is known as "Bear #2" because she is the very first person in my life to ask what I was doing and follow my lead. I was only down about 70 pounds (32 kg) at that time, and Anna was feeling a bit desperate because she was facing medication for diabetes and has a family tree completely filled with complicated cases. It was sometime in late October that she asked me about it. I received an excited text message from her over the Christmas holiday season, telling me she no longer needed the diabetes medication. She has lost about 40 pounds (18 kg) and looks radiant. Her family

noticed, and many have followed her lead, as have friends and other moms at school.

In Anna's excitement, she talked to another school mom, Lisa, a Type 2 diabetes case with neuropathy in her feet at only fifty years old. In response to Anna's testimony, Lisa implemented the plan and, like many people in the group, has improved her hemoglobin A1C level, is off all medications, and has improved feeling in her feet. She has lost 30 pounds (14 kg) and has changed her health completely.

Located in California's diabetes capital, we hope that many people will follow Anna and Lisa's lead.

Not to be outdone, across the country in central Pennsylvania is Jackie Patti, a trained biochemist, obsessed with numbers and measures, who was also planning her final days (very literally) when she started this. She may be one of the more obvious Lazarus cases in the group.

I have been friends with Jackie online for many years and knew she had serious health problems, but when I saw her go on a trip to her hometown this past spring, I was excited that she was finally able to get out after being shut in for some time. What I did not realize, even as a good reader of tea leaves on social media, is that she was visiting her hometown one last time, saying good-bye, knowing she probably did not have another year to live. Her dad died at this age, and her own diabetes-related complications continued to worsen. She could not walk due to lymphedema and worsening neuropathy below her knees. An avid and long-time gardener, Jackie gave away all of her gardening tools this past summer, closing the door on that chapter of her life. She could not walk to the porch to look at her garden, much less actually garden. She no longer had a need for gardening tools.

When Jackie joined the group, she was on 100 units of insulin daily. Jackie leveraged stretches of extended fasts following the advice of Jason Fung, M.D. She appreciates the nutrient density of the Ridiculously Big Salad and relies on it between bouts of multiday fasting. Jackie no longer requires insulin, and she walks daily in her garden with her cats. She calls her walks "the walks with the kitties," and we see the kitties prancing joyfully through the field as their patron follows behind them, walking for the first time in years, with her fabulous blue hair.

Jackie updates the community regularly on her progress and is definitely one to follow via her community posts and her blog. She is only four months in as I write this and only 20 pounds (9 kg) down due to a more complicated health history, but the community is electrified by her story as her new life emerges.

Although we have known each other for years, it took Jackie more than a year to join our group. She thought I had gone nuts and had started some sort of anorexic cult, and she wanted no part of it. She is likely more jaded and sarcastic than I was back in 2017, but when she did decide to jump in, she jumped pretty big, likely saving her own life, which was evident in *months,* and even weeks.

In "A Postcard from Yellowstone" I ask, "*What if you lifted that hammer one more time, how much might your life change?*" I look forward to your story.

If you can launch yourself out of the
fiery pit, on your *own strength*, your internal
transformation is likely to be far more *powerful*
than what you can contemplate at this moment.

Transformations and

NSV and true victory example of this WOE....outdoor movie night on the asphalt with blanket, and I could criss-cross applesauce through the entire movie with my 8 year old grandson using me as a backrest. I was so comfortable and no pain. I would never been able to do that before this journey. The weight coming off has so many benefits that truly improve quality of life. I often wonder how I stumbled on **Amanda Rose**'s feed - but that day changed my life for the better. 🙏

NSV (???) 🚶 On this gorgeous fall evening, I went to walk around our lake downtown in the same cotton shorts I've worn for years. Halfway through the crosswalk, cars stopped in both directions, the weight of my phone in my pocket caused my pants to fall off!!! 🤣 It was a very public NSV! 🙈 Guess it's time for smaller pants. (30+ lbs and counting.)

Nsv.....getting in and out of an armed chair without sitting at an angle or just sitting on the front edge! Oh and not taking the chair with you when getting up!

Non-Scale Victory Moments

NSV!!!

SOMEONE PINCH ME!!! I'm in a fitting room at American Eagle!!!

I have gone from a size 24 (gettin snug) to a size 12!!
Let me say that again A SIZE 12!!
I have never worn a size 12, well maybe in middle school!!
On my 5'8" frame this is beyond a MIRACLE!!!

WoooHooo
30 more lbs to go-ish and I can't believe I DID IT!!! I AM DOING IT!!

Non scale victory for me! I have never been a runner. I also hate cold weather. This morning I ran the Hot Chocolate 5k Race in St. Louis, MO! It was a cold one for sure at 17 degrees & with the wind chill it felt like 9 degrees but I DID IT!

NSV!! I just realized I have a space between me and the steering wheel... Lol. It's the little things!! 70 pounds makes a huge difference. So happy today!!

PART ONE

WHEN, WHAT, WHY, HOW

chapter one

When and What to Eat

I am going to admit that there is nothing really revolutionary in these pages, and yet they may just change your life. If you have a whole lot of weight to lose, and you follow my lead, you are going to be eating a salad most days over the course of a year or longer. To lose weight, I ate a Ridiculously Big Salad about every four out of five days for about a year. I ate it once a day, and that is all I ate. It is that simple. In maintenance, I find myself doing the same. You would think I would be tired of the salads, but I continue to crave them. The structure simply works for me. I am more satisfied and less likely to binge on more calories or junk if my stomach is digesting a huge bowl of salad greens.

To eat this type of salad nearly every day, giving your body the rest it needs to burn fat and giving your palate the variety it probably craves, the salads need to be simple, and they need to be different from one another.

In some cases, you may be juggling food for other people under your roof, your work is stressful, or you may be physically limited and unable to spend a lot of time standing in your kitchen. The fact is, most of us are already under water in our kitchen tasks, and the winning strategy is to keep all of this as simple as possible.

This little book is all about a shockingly simple and effective model for weight loss and lifelong health. I will deconstruct the Ridiculously Big Salad and give you a very simple approach to mix and match the three core parts of the salad.

Over a six-week period you will taste many different salad dressings along with a variety of protein toppers. In the process, you will find favorites that you may choose to eat more often. You will find combinations that you enjoy and that are easy for you to implement, and you will use them as your own go-to salad options.

However, to understand a bit better why the Ridiculously Big Salad works so ridiculously well for weight loss, consider that it falls under two popular weight-loss frameworks: intermittent fasting and the ketogenic diet. Finally, consider why it may be the most effective subclass of these two popular trends.

WHEN TO EAT: INTERMITTENT FASTING

Over the decades of my life, it simply never occurred to me that "when to eat" could change my life, and yet here we are. I consider "when to eat" the game-changing element for me in this weight-loss program. The term intermittent fasting includes the word fasting because there is a time period in the day (or set of days) when you do not eat. You have a window of time in which you eat, and you have a period of fasting in which you do not eat. It is that simple. The shorter the window of eating, the greater your weight loss is likely to be. You will eat your salad in about an hour (although some people eat it over a few hours), and then you will stop eating until you eat another salad tomorrow.

Note in figure 1, "A Day in the Life of Intermittent Fasting," a wheel, mostly blue, representing a twenty-four-hour period. One small portion of the wheel is green. That green portion is the one-hour part of the day when you eat your salad. The entire rest of the day, the blue portion, is when you do not eat or drink *anything* that affects your blood sugar.

This is an intensive weight-loss strategy, the one I used. However, it is highly flexible and adaptable. My husband ate two meals in five hours and lost 15 pounds (7 kg) in a month. He ate a breakfast of eggs and sausage at about 9:00 a.m. and then a Ridiculously Big Salad at about 1:00 p.m., finishing by 2:00 p.m. His eating was started and completed in

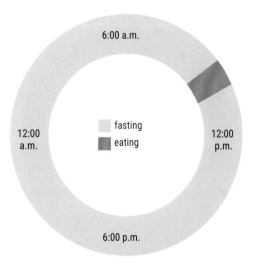

FIGURE 1: A Day In the Life of Intermittent Fasting

five hours, until the next day when his eating began again. The model worked well for him, as a man who only had about 30 pounds (14 kg) to lose. I needed a much more intensive strategy, which led to eating a Ridiculously Big Salad in one hour. The structure is adaptable.

I began this way of eating without a plan, and, as it worked, I started to wonder why it was so effective. Months later I found the writing of Canadian nephrologist Jason Fung, M.D., author of *The Obesity Code* and *The Diabetes Code*. If you are overweight, read the former. If you are also diabetic, read the latter. He has helped popularize the idea of intermittent fasting for weight loss and is likely one reason my friends online were stirring about intermittent fasting, causing me to give it a try.

Fung tells a compelling story of the rise in obesity rates in America, as driven by the combined impact of the carbohydrate-heavy food pyramid, the growing snack culture, and the "six little meals" recommendation, popular among mainstream nutritionists. Both practices cause your body to produce insulin more often throughout the day. You eat a bunch of little meals every day, and, each time, your body produces insulin. With each meal, soda, coffee with cream and sugar, cocktail, and handful of nuts, your body produces insulin. Slowly, over time, your body needs to produce more insulin to have the same effect because it is also slowly building up a resistance to the insulin it is producing. As a result, we end up with increasing levels of insulin in our blood. With insulin in our blood, we cannot burn off our stored body fat. If we could just get our insulin levels down long enough to burn off some of that body fat, we could really start hammering away at our problem.

What if instead of eating six little meals and producing insulin six separate times, we eat one *ridiculously big* meal, low in carbohydrates and high in fiber? Our bodies would produce insulin once, and we would have more hours for our insulin levels to go down and allow our body to burn its stored fat. It turns out there is some magic in that model, and it is why I encourage you to eat only once a day if you are able. Eat a ridiculous, fiber-loaded quantity to get yourself to tomorrow.

WHAT TO EAT: "KETO" (OR THE LOW-CARB PLAN OF YOUR CHOICE)

The Ridiculously Big Salad is a ketogenic meal, but it's far from the keto stereotype in America today. I tell people that in my one hour of eating a day I follow a keto diet, and their reaction is animated: "Keto is soooo unhealthy!"

People have a knee-jerk reaction to the word *keto* because they picture me eating a plate of sausage and eggs for the rest of my life, like an entire life on the Atkins induction diet. I find that if I do not use the word *keto* and simply show people a picture of my food, no one expresses concern for my health over what I am eating. They might be shocked that I can eat such a giant salad, but they are not concerned that the salad is unhealthy.

From the other side, some proponents in the hard-core keto community would have me carefully measure my fat and protein, using apps to optimize them, and are a bit horrified that I do not measure anything.

What I call my meals, how I measure them, and whether I optimize them in some way is far less important to me than these questions: Am I actually healthier today than I was one year ago? Can I walk?

Cut out high-sugar and high-starch foods, because these will raise your insulin levels like no other foods will. If you adopt the Ridiculously Big Salad framework and eat that way for months, you will likely be in ketosis for months, burning the fat right off your body. In ketosis, your body switches from using sugars to energize your body to using fat instead. Because you are also keeping your insulin levels low, your body has more ready access to your stored fat, a powerful thing if you are keeping your calories on the low side.

Some people get concerned about the long-term consequences of a keto diet — of being in ketosis forever. This notion is a barrier to getting started, but, as an argument, it is a red herring. You do not have to stay in ketosis for the rest of your life, but if you have a lot of pounds to lose, you may choose to stay in it for many months. Decide later if you want to be in ketosis forever. Whatever the case, as I mentioned in the prologue, you may not be the same person a year from now. Let your future self decide how to handle maintenance.

That new person will have much more wisdom about what is best for you moving forward.

In the meantime, do not let naysayers today distract you from your goal for tomorrow. You can follow my lead: turn off the internet chatter, eat a salad, and go outside for fresh air.

WHY A SALAD (AND NOT A PLATE OF BACON AND EGGS)

There are some great scientific reasons that the Ridiculously Big Salad worked so well, but I will admit that I lucked into it completely. If you know my story, you probably know that I jumped into the one-meal-a-day model with no real plan, following no guru or framework. In fact, I thought all of the weight-loss programs out there were complete garbage (and, the fact is, most are). In the very beginning, with no plan and simply fueled by desperation, I went on an extended fast, drinking only electrolyte water; broke the fast with a soup filled with greens; and then added solid food back in, but eating only one meal a day.

I had never been much of a salad-eater, certainly not as you might expect, given the Ridiculously Big Salad model, but I suspect that as I laid on the couch on my water fast, thinking about my future one meal a day, I thought to myself: "If I am only going to eat once, I am not going to fool around!" At the same time, I knew that binging on calories in that meal would not get me where I needed to be. Some fifteen years ago, I read Joel Fuhrman's book *Eat to Live*. He is a vegan weight-loss guru who emphasizes the nutrient density of greens, on a calorie basis. Basically, you can pack a lot of nutrition into 100 calories with the lettuce and cabbage approach. My guess is that, somewhere in my subconscious, as I laid on the couch getting through my extended fast, I actually channeled a bit of Joel Fuhrman, an ironic thing considering that I am about as far from a vegan as a person can be. Some six months into the diet, I found Dr. Eric Berg's keto diet empire on YouTube and his strong recommendation to eat 7 to 10 cups (1.5 to 2 liters) of vegetables a day — certainly a recommendation leaning toward the salad approach and away from the keto stereotype of bacon and eggs.

In any case, during that water fast I wanted to chew on something, but I did not want to pack in the calories. Chew I did. It takes an hour to chew a Ridiculously Big Salad. I allowed myself one hour to do so, a reason I tell people that "I ate one meal a day in one hour to lose 100 pounds (45 kg) in eight months and 140 pounds (64 kg) total."

I limited myself to one hour because I needed a boundary. Had I allowed myself five hours, I would have had many more temptations each day. I probably would have had less success because a good bit more food would have snuck into those five hours. Although my reasons were psychological, the boundary had an effect on my insulin level and on my whole suite of fat-burning hormones as a result.

Some people might not be able to eat this whole salad in one hour. They may need two or three hours instead. Some people eat it in two meals over five hours. Whichever model works for you is exactly the model you should be implementing, but I personally find it harder to break it up because, over the course of five hours, I could convince myself to snack on many other things because, you know, "*I feel hungry.*" (Those hunger feelings are hormonal. I always feel hungry and want to eat if I allow my mind to dwell on it.)

Although I considered none of this as I got started, in retrospect I have some appreciation for why this model of eating worked so well for me. It turns out that chewing a Ridiculously Big Salad for an hour has some benefits.

- **You will naturally restrict your caloric intake for the day.** The one-meal model does that, but so does the giant bowl of greens you are eating. If you really eat all of those greens (and you should), you simply have less room in your stomach for other things. If you are ravenously seeking dessert after your *Ridiculously Big Salad*, your salad needs to be *ridiculously bigger.*
- **You may naturally moderate your protein intake.** There are arguments that too much protein impedes weight loss, although the jury is still out on this issue. It is a claim I do not spend time thinking about, because with my framework you are filling much of your stomach with greens, and you therefore cannot over-

eat protein. You can still get plenty of protein: I tend to eat about "two decks of cards" worth of protein on my salads, roughly 6 ounces (180 grams) of protein if a deck is 3 ounces (85 grams). There are some days that I probably eat a whopping half pound (8 ounces, 230 grams) on my salad, as I feel hungry for more protein.

- **You will reduce your insulin levels.** You are simply not spiking your blood sugar throughout the day, allowing your insulin levels to come down. It turns out that this is important in helping your body burn more fat and a big reason the one meal, the Ridiculously Big Salad, works so well for so many of us.

- **You will eat a lot of fiber.** Fiber has a lot of potential health benefits. We all know that it keeps us "regular." It also helps with blood sugar levels. It may help reduce blood pressure and inflammation. However, here is a powerful benefit for our purposes: The amount of fiber in a giant bowl of greens takes hours to digest and will pack your stomach with a feeling of fullness that no plate of eggs and sausage can. We have this stereotypical way of thinking in the ketogenic diet world that fullness comes from fat and protein. However, on the days I skip my salad, I feel less full and less satisfied. I am sure that the huge amount of fiber in the salad is a big reason for this. I manage my hunger on my Ridiculously Big Salad days far better, as a result.

- **You will chew a whole lot.** We have been told to chew our food well so that we get more nutrition from the food and so that we are more satisfied with our meals. The act of chewing has benefits. Eggs and sausage require far less chewing than a Ridiculously Big Salad. You simply cannot eat a Ridiculously Big Salad without a lot of chewing, giving it another structural advantage.

- **You will take your time to eat.** Taking time and allowing our bodies to feast in a more leisurely manner encourages the positive act of chewing and may also help our bodies to be more satisfied with that meal. There is no way to eat this massive bowl of salad without taking time. There are no shortcuts. If the Ridiculously Big Salad is what you are eating, you are taking time to do so, and that time may provide its own benefits.

THE WHAT: THE PARTS OF THE RIDICULOUSLY BIG SALAD

The Ridiculously Big Salad has three parts that I consider to be required and a fourth that is optional, for flavor and variety.

1. **Greens.** This is just the romaine, cabbage, spinach, iceberg lettuce, butter leaf lettuce, red leaf lettuce, or other green that you use as your base. Use them all, if you like. Use the same green every day. Use whatever you can get. Whatever you do, use a lot of greens. This is a key winning strategy. You want the greens to fill your stomach like it is a holiday feast. The greens will supply you with many micronutrients and will fill your stomach with very few calories.

2. **Salad Dressing.** Most of the flavor of your meal and the calories are in this part of the salad. In my opinion, the dressing is how you are going to survive for a year or longer eating this type of meal almost every day. If you cook your protein in bulk, as I describe later in this book, your daily meal preparation will mostly involve making salad dressings. Luckily for us, they are very simple to make.

3. **A Protein Topper.** This is meat, eggs, or cheese that is going to supply you with protein and fat. It will, of course, add calories as well. You will mix and match your proteins with your greens and your dressings. Later in this book, I give you my key strategies on having these protein toppers on hand at all times, requiring only minutes of preparation.

4. **"Other stuff."** The Ridiculously Big Salad actually has a fourth part — "other stuff" — but I see it as optional, just helping us get some extra flavor variation and perhaps a bit of crunch or nutrition. This is where you add onion, bell pepper, cheese,

roasted nuts, and more, all mindful of the calories and carbo-hydrates in what you are adding.

You will find many examples in this book to help you fine-tune the Ridiculously Big Salad in your life.

RIDICULOUSLY BIG SALAD QUALITIES

In the meantime, there are some general elements of implementation that are worthy of note, salad details that are likely important.

- **Fresh.** Nearly all of my salads were homemade with fresh ingredients. The salads were not certified organic or anything otherwise fancy. Gourmet items may have appeared in them at various times. Sometimes I use greens from the forest around me, but most salads just contain regular old produce. My most intensive period of weight loss was in the fall and winter when my access to fancier stuff was more limited, probably an important lesson that "fancy" matters less than simply "fresh" and "whole."
- **Quality ingredients.** I make 98 percent or more of my salad dressings myself. I have not eaten a store-bought salad dressing in many months. I eat dressings at restaurants on occasion, accounting for the other 2 percent. Controling the ingredients of your dressing may be an important success factor when you are eating salad dressing nearly every day and when that dressing makes up a big proportion of your fat and calorie intake.
- **Whole foods.** My protein toppers and other salad parts are whole-food-based. My diet has never been particularly high in processed or packaged foods. I do have some processed meat products on my salads at times, but you can see from the recipes in this book that they are fairly limited. The only real exceptions are cured bacon, lunch meat, and canned tuna, all

of which I consider well balanced by all of the freshness of the salad greens.

- **Low carbohydrate and calorie-mindful.** My salads have always been calorie-mindful as well as carb-mindful. In the keto world, we are trained to count carbohydrates, but as I worked on this salad book and took a look at my salads again with fresh eyes, I definitely learned how mindful I have been about calories. The fact is that you can load a whole bunch of calories on top of a salad with cheese, nuts, and avocados, in particular, just as you can add to the carbs with too many tomatoes or blueberries. As I made my salads all over again for this book, I realized that when I added nuts to them, I did not tend to add cheese and avocado. When I added avocado, I did not tend to add nuts and cheese. These are keto-approved salad toppings, but you can still overeat them and end up eating more calories than you ought to if you need to lose a lot of weight.

OTHER LIFESTYLE SUCCESS STRUCTURES

In addition to what you put in your salad bowl, some other lifestyle structures may be very important for us.

- **Earlier-in-the-day eating.** I eat my salads usually around 10 a.m., but pretty much always by 1 p.m. The separation of my eating from my sleeping at night may be an important factor. Your body has plenty of hours to work on digesting, so that when you go to sleep, it can use its energy to burn your fat and to repair itself. Digestion takes a lot of energy, and our body focuses on the work of digesting when we give it food. It focuses on fat-burning and on repair when we give it a break from digesting. People speculate that my excellent skin outcome is due to this time for repair, attributing my skin improvement since the weight loss to a process called "auto-phagy," perhaps a happy side benefit of all of this. That said, we have people in our community eating their meal later in the day and are making good progress. Whatever you implement, it needs to work within the structure of your lifestyle.

- **Mental focus.** When I got started on my extended fast and then jumped into one meal a day with the Ridiculously Big Salad, that is all I did. I made it my full-time job. I actually told my family that for the month of September 2017, "Mama's services are closed. I will be laying on the couch, probably grumpy, and you may disturb me only if the house is on fire." I had never done such a thing before in my life. My kids survived, although it is not as if I had toddlers in the house. My husband, an actual adult, who way back in college and grad school fixed his own food for himself, conjured up his past life and made it through. (He is actually very supportive. I am lucky.) It was a good experience for all of us. By dialing in and focusing, I made tremendous progress in my weight loss, to the tune of a life-changing half a pound (0.23 kg) a day. When that month was over, I had serious momentum and kept fighting for that focus. I skipped my college reunion at about the five-week point because I knew it might get me off track. I suppose that might seem sad, but I am not sad about it at all. I made the right decision for my long-term health. I wonder what might have happened had I let myself lose momentum, especially right before the holidays, in my particular case.

- **I slept a lot and kept my workload low.** Before the diet, I would often get up by 5:00 a.m. and work while the household was quiet. But during these intensive months, I had very low expectations for any work or productivity and focused on rest. Allowing myself that luxury produced something I had not expected: I slept a lot, far more than I even realized was possible. My body seemed to be craving sleep, and I let myself sleep when I could. I slept for ten hours some nights, like a rock. Some days I would wake up at 5:00 a.m., use the bathroom, do an obsessive weight check, go back to sleep for two hours, and then weigh in again. It was crazy because sometimes that

second weigh-in was less than the first. That in itself encour-
aged me to go back to sleep: *"Maybe I'll lose half a pound!"*
Your weight can fluctuate a lot, so who knows what was going
on, but all of that sleep must have produced benefits. My body
could focus on burning fat and on repairing itself.

- **The initial water fast.** As I see more people implementing the salad
  approach and I get more feedback on implementation from
  medical professionals, quite a few people have pointed to my
  initial water fast as a success factor. The feedback makes me
  think that anyone who can medically manage a two-day or
  three-day water fast to jump-start themselves should do so.
  That said, do not freak out at my particular story — you will
  see evidence of my desperation in the fact that I jump-started
  my salad-eating days with a two-week water fast in which I
  drank nothing but water and electrolyte drinks. I had an intra-
  venous vitamin and mineral treatment from my primary care
  doctor one week in. That is it. I chewed nothing. I did not
  even drink coffee. The two-week fast may have actually made
  my implementation of the Ridiculously Big Salad easier than
  we might expect. Fasting does powerful things for feelings of
  hunger. Your hormones get under control, and you get your
  body out of the habit of thinking it needs to eat every few
  hours. When you finally eat again, you are so pleased to be in
  the salad game that you hardly miss the muffins or the cocktails. You certainly are in a ketogenic, fat-burning mode.

Throughout my eight months of intensive weight loss and even today
in maintenance, I do a forty-eight- or seventy-two-hour fast as a bit of a
diet reset — after a big event or a period of stress. The reset helps bring
all of those fat-burning hormones into balance.

I see people struggling for months to move from three meals a day
to one meal a day and wonder if they could cut right to it by doing
an extended fast over a long holiday weekend. The go-to resource on
the topic of extended fasting is Canadian nephrologist Jason Fung, M.D.,
author of *The Complete Guide to Fasting* and *The Obesity Code.*

If you could teleport yourself to March 2017, I might look a lot like you do now. I am not the same "me" today as I was when I was down in that pit. Do not look at my confidence as the *cause* of my success. It is, rather, the *result*.

BREAKING THE NIGHTTIME HABIT

I found this trick quite by accident, and you can replicate it with intent.

As I faced the desperation of needing to lose all of that weight, I realized the harsh reality that probably half or more of my weight came right out of the bottle — I drank a nightly cocktail, or two. I made gourmet herbal mixers, and I could not imagine giving them up. I struggled so much with the decision that I realized how addicted I had become to that drink.

I was able to give the alcohol up when I started the diet, but my concern was for the long term: If I had a bad circumstance in my life, what would keep me from lapsing into the old habit? I did not have an answer to that question, and it did concern me. I forged ahead with the weight loss anyway.

Why was nightly drinking such a big deal and at a high risk of relapse? As with any habit, we have a cue that triggers a routine of some sort, and that routine is followed by a reward. For nighttime drinkers, our cue happens every single day: Day becomes night, and we prepare for sleep. We grab our cocktail as part of our routine, and we are rewarded with flavor and relaxation. Over many years, we need to drink more to maintain the reward of relaxation, and we may find, over some decades, that we are drinking a lot and that we may be chemically dependent on it as well. For me, in the shorter term, the drink was also making me fat.

Some six weeks into the diet and down 40 pounds (18 kg), I had lost so much fat and fluid in my face that my neck wrinkles were pretty shocking. In response, I made high-end customized skin oils, using some of my favorite herbs. I blended up about three parts jojoba oil to one part pomegranate seed oil in a 2-ounce (60 ml) bottle. I added a couple of drops of rose geranium essential oil and about 10 drops of rose absolute.

This combination both soothed my senses and supported my skin. I applied the blend liberally with a focus on my neck. I kept a bottle by the bedside so that I would never forget to apply it.

About six weeks into my skin regimen, I was tossing and turning a bit one night. I had applied the oil an hour before, but I reached for it again, and as I pulled it toward me and the aroma caught my nose, I took in its fragrance greedily and then I applied it to my neck. My physical response to the fragrance surprised me, and I realized that I was craving the aroma of that oil blend. I had replaced the craving of alcohol with a new craving.

This area of our necks that gets awfully wrinkly also happens to be a primary receptor for aromatherapy. I was creating a new, powerful habit by accident. If I manage never to drink a cocktail at night again, I may actually win this battle against alcohol.

Beyond alcohol, this concept can be applied to any difficult nighttime habit, the skin oil idea itself or other nighttime rituals that are better for your health than alcohol and snacks.

chapter two

Focus, Discipline, and Maintenance

It sounds straight-up crazy to eat a Ridiculously Big Salad nearly every day for a year. I am sure that in my first year of eating this way I ate more lettuce than in the previous forty-plus years of my life. What is crazy is that I am still eating the salads because the framework simply works. I do not feel as satisfied without them. In fact, I have come to crave them.

The rest of this book will show you how you, too, can follow this highly effective framework for months on end without getting bored. I will admit, it is a grind, and you will always want to eat the bad stuff, but it will not be from lack of flavor. However, while the food and eating framework is a necessary condition for success, it is not sufficient. Making this change is a complete head game. You need to batten the hatches and bring your best strategies to bear.

THE FOCUS AND DISCIPLINE TO IMPLEMENT

This weight-loss plan is very simple. However, it is anything but easy. If you are losing more than 100 pounds (45 kg), it is the grind of your life. It is long and tiring, and however fast it might go, you will yearn for it to go at least two times faster. If you are in the Eat Like a Bear! community on Facebook, you will find someone weeks ahead of you and 25 pounds (11 kg) beyond you, and you will feel a tinge of jealousy. That is simply how it is.

However, the crazy thing about it is that those months are going to pass anyway, and if you keep your head down and do it, those months will go by, and you will end up as metamorphosed rock rather than as a pile of decomposed granite. I remember the grind, but in retrospect, the grind feels like such a small investment for a strikingly huge reward.

Granted, I have that perspective here on the other side, and you are still living in the land of an uncertain payoff, which is why I suggest that you make a small, two-week test of this model. If it works, you can bring your lifelong discipline and focus to bear on the problem and just hammer on this thing until you are done. If it does not work, you can cut and run. (Actually, if it really does not seem to be working after a week or so, get feedback from our community before you completely cut and run, especially if you have more complex medical conditions. We have many community members with Type 2 diabetes and autoimmune diseases who are making great health progress but losing weight a bit more slowly due to those health conditions and perhaps due to the related medications. Their cases may provide you with some knowledge to take to your doctor.)

Basically, if this works for you anywhere near as well as it has worked for me, your success will fuel your discipline. Following are the principles that helped me lose weight and that keep me successful in maintenance:

- **Jump in. Once you have momentum, success will fuel your discipline.** We have group members who take months to get started as they line up their life or their minds to get into the groove. I had to line up some ducks, as well, to get started. However, we also have people who are laid up on the couch, needing a change, who struggle with jumping in because they are just not sure it will work. They are not sure if this way of eating is sustainable, or they are just not sure they can do it. They waste time and energy wondering, squandering that couch time. I spent nine months on the couch before I really got started. Of course, I had no plan at all. Take two weeks and implement this plan rather than two weeks wondering about it (or two months or two years). Your best data collection will happen in implementation, not in wondering.

- **Make food rules daily, but make them the night before.** Choice is a great thing, and we should all have some freedom to choose, but when it comes to eating, decisions are best made when we are strong, and that happens to be when temptation is not in front of us. If I allow myself to choose in the moment of temptation, I am likely to make a very bad decision. Rather than fight with that problem every single minute of the day, I make decisions the night before about what I will do the next day. During the long diet grind, my default decision for the next day was usually something like this: "I will eat one ketogenic meal without dessert in about an hour."

The rule was that simple, and I did not break it. If I knew that I might have an extra dinner due to some special event, my rule might have been: "I will eat a ketogenic lunch and a light ketogenic dinner at the event." I went on occasional seventy-two-hour water fasts, and my rule was easier still: "I will not eat tomorrow."

I cannot overstate how important it is to stay true to the rules that you make. Make them to give yourself the flexibility you need, but then do not break them.

One day about a year into my maintenance, I had a very bad day and really wanted to eat something that evening. My eating period was over, and eating at that point would have broken the rule. The devil on my shoulder whispered, "You are in maintenance. A snack will not matter. You *deserve* it." I was ready to break the rule. I took a step back and wondered, "Is this the moment where it all falls apart? Did you come this far over the past two years only to break your commitment, all for a little snack?" Breaking the rules, not being true to yourself, is like a swan dive right back into the pit. Make your rules and follow them.

(No, I did not eat the snack.)

- **You are always either in weight-loss mode or you are honing your maintenance skills.** "Weight-loss mode" and "honing maintenance" are the two modes for the rest of your life, so get started on your series of new habits right now. There is no "falling off the wagon" unless getting on and off the wagon is part of the new habit you are seeking to foster. If you are going on a vacation or to a big event, make a rule for yourself that will keep you reasonably on track so that you can just keep going afterward. Decide to eat in a larger window of time and to add a few carbs. This is not "cheating" or "falling off the wagon." This is simply behavior management.

However, I will add that it is easier in the beginning to stay completely focused, strict, and on track, even if that means eating before an event and then, at the event, only eating the steak or shrimp or whatever low-carbohydrate food they might be serving. It is very important in the beginning to preserve your momentum.

- **Do not veer from the goal.** This may be the longest grind of your life, and it is to your great advantage to jump in and get the grind behind you, in one long, continuous stretch of daily decisions. Something powerful happens when you do something every single day for a year or longer, right through vacations and holiday dinners, persevering through the daily challenges that will tempt you to veer from your goal. Do not veer. Stay the course. Collect your benefit: A powerful new lifestyle habit. Collect it and hold on to it. You earned it.

- **Write down your intentions and your focus every day.** There are many approaches to intentional writing or journaling, a process that helps you to keep your head in the game and to stay focused on your goals. Writing your goals daily in some way will help you do that. Make sure you find an approach that works for you. The purpose in the context of weight loss is to keep your mind engaged on your goal so that you can push through and make the decisions you need to make. The focus in itself is a discipline that will help you build new habits and a new life. Do not underestimate the role of intention and the value of writing to reinforce it.

That said, everyone will have a different approach. Many group members write daily affirmations about their character or other personal traits. I do not write affirmations. Rather,

I write words of focus. I write the word *walk* not to remind me to get out on a daily walk, but as a reminder of my darkest days when I could not. After having written this book, I might write *fire*, *pressure*, or *grind*, the critical catalysts for life transformation.

MAINTENANCE

As I write this book, I have maintained my weight loss for more than a year and a half. I do not consider myself a maintenance success story and will not likely consider myself a success for at least forty years. That said, I have now maintained my weight longer, with more ease, than I have in my previous fifty years.

I thought an awful lot about "the maintenance problem" as I began this diet. I often tell people about a diet I started on July 4, 2016, that lasted an entire day and a half. About midday on July 5, I asked myself, "How will you maintain your weight loss *this time*?" I was astounded by the question and by my lack of an answer. Rather than put more energy into a weight-loss diet, I stopped the diet and turned my focus to identifying maintenance factors and structures, a process that found me weeks later hiking with my sons in Cedar Breaks, Utah; Sedona, Arizona; and finally Palm Springs, California, where I busted my knee and found myself laid up on my couch, making an appointment with a bariatric surgeon. As I laid on the couch, wondering if I could even lose the weight, I was highly concerned about whether I could ever maintain it. Bariatric surgery offered a new solution for weight loss, but even bariatric surgery patients end up right back where they started. I did feel a frantic pain about "the maintenance question."

I remembered that feeling a few months ago as life got stressful and I was spending too much time sitting at a computer, ironically working on the first draft of this book. I asked myself: "What if all of this stress and sitting makes you FAT?" That frantic voice was always such a core part of me since July 5, 2016. "How will you maintain your weight *this time*?" My panic stemmed from those days, but my response came from a different place: "You can walk. If you gain, you can grind it off." My fear was gone, replaced not by arrogance and overconfidence but by a mindfulness of the tools I could employ to solve the problem. Indeed, at 140 pounds (63 kg) and with a plan, there are far more options to lose and maintain weight. A rigorous hike is worth about a pound (0.45 kg). I can walk, and I can eat a bit less. If I can simply catch it while I can still fit into my pants, I have won. It is what we have always been told to do, but I simply did not have any history of success with it, until now.

WHAT I EAT TODAY

All that said, I have had success in maintenance so far because I have continued to do what I did all those months in weight-loss mode, albeit loosened up just a bit. I watch the carbohydrates or calories, but not quite as much.

To lose the weight, my daily intake was 1,000 to 1,200 calories. These days, I often eat a Ridiculously Big Salad perhaps with some additional toppings or a small entrée like a stuffed pepper or a small omelet, to the tune of 1,800 calories. In weight-loss mode, I kept my daily net grams of carbohydrates in the 20 to 30 range. In maintenance I do not count, but my daily carbohydrates are likely still under 40 net grams. More than half of my days in maintenance I have eaten in about a five-hour window. I have had a handful of eight-hour window days. Increasingly, I am gravitating back to three hours as I get increasing feedback that a shorter window of eating is a great long-term health strategy, a point you will notice if you find my "loose skin" video on YouTube. When I am doing a lot of heavier gardening work or going on longer hikes, I do eat a bit more over a period of about five hours.

In all of these months, I maintain my mental structure of "make my eating decisions the night before." My default rule right now is "I will eat a ketogenic meal, and maybe a bit more, in three hours."

Whatever my daily rule is in maintenance, I do not break it.

I write *walk* in my daily journal as short-form for this: Remember when you couldn't walk and now *you can.*

The RBS-Maker's Tool Kit

chapter three

The Parts of the Ridiculously Big Salad (RBS)

The Ridiculously Big Salad has three core parts and an optional fourth part for added flavor and texture. This chapter is designed to give you an overview of putting these parts together. I have introduced each already, but this discussion will give you a little more intuition for your goal as you build salads and make them your own.

SALAD PART 1. THE GREENS: LOTS AND LOTS, FRESH AND WHOLE

Your very best strategy for winning with the greens portion of your salad is to eat a variety of them, whatever you have access to. In the graph shown in figure 2, note that your best strategy may be to choose the greens at the top of a nutrient list, such as this antioxidant list. A giant red leaf lettuce or purple cauliflower salad will win the day, if you can find these vegetables.

The graph displays the oxygen radical absorbance capacity (ORAC) value of greens collected by the United States Department of Agriculture (USDA). The ORAC value is a test-tube measure of a food's potential ability to combat cancer-causing free radicals. The measure is a bit outdated, but the graph tells a story many different nutrient graphs would tell: Some greens have far more nutrients than others.

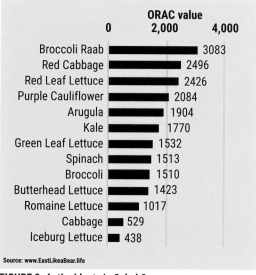

Source: www.EastLikeaBear.life

FIGURE 2: Antioxidents in Salad Greens

That said, it is easy to make this complicated and to go out and try to hunt down all of the greens in the universe, just to give yourself an edge. If you enjoy the hunt, you should definitely go hunting. If your time is limited, and all you can find in the grocery store is romaine, iceberg, and cabbage, you have all you need to eat like this for a year or longer.

For eight weeks, as I worked on this book, I ate salads every day with greens at the very bottom of this antioxidant list — iceberg, romaine, and green cabbage. I felt great.

This is my strong belief: You just need to eat the greens that you can find, that you like, and that you can afford. If you make things too complicated or try to eat greens you do not enjoy, you will not maintain this way of eating over the long term, and you will not win the game as a result.

Stepping It Up

If you do not love some of those more nutritious greens or if you do not have them readily available, you can step up your salads by adding nutrition and flavor in the form of herbs and spices. What your iceberg lettuce may lack, you can find in another leaf and add it to your salad greens or, perhaps even better, add it to your salad dressing.

A few salad dressings in this book feature herbs. Those recipes are highly adaptable to any herb you might want to play with on your salads. Go through this basic list first and discover what is working for you — what recipes you like to eat and what is easiest for you to manage. As you become more comfortable with your routine, I encourage you to venture out into some of these other flavors. You might even find some growing wild in your area. There is no telling what experiences and adventures await you as you seek out all of the great flavors of the plant world.

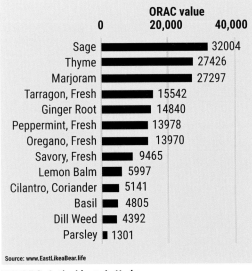

ORAC value

Sage	32004
Thyme	27426
Marjoram	27297
Tarragon, Fresh	15542
Ginger Root	14840
Peppermint, Fresh	13978
Oregano, Fresh	13970
Savory, Fresh	9465
Lemon Balm	5997
Cilantro, Coriander	5141
Basil	4805
Dill Weed	4392
Parsley	1301

Source: www.EastLikeaBear.life

FIGURE 3: Antioxidents in Herbs

By the way, the scale on the herb graph in figure 3 is ten times the scale on the lettuce graph. These herbs are nutritional powerhouses.

SALAD PART 2. THE FAT AND FLAVOR OF THE SALAD DRESSING

The dressings on my salads average 450 calories and 50 grams of fat. This is not your mama's 1995 low-fat salad dressing. The fat will help you feel more satisfied with your meal, and it will carry flavor to every leaf of your salad. Add a bit less to your salad than I do, and if you are satisfied, you will shave a few calories off your meal. You can also tinker with the proportions to reduce the calories — add more yogurt than mayonnaise, for example. Add more vinegar than oil. Calories still matter, and you will simply lose faster if you keep your calories in check.

Keep in mind, too, that this core part of the salad not only brings you important nutrition, but the flavor of your salad will live or die right in this layer as well. You can pack a serious amount of flavor into these dressings. The recipes in this book are your starting point, but turn them up to your heart's content. This part of the salad is probably the top reason I am still eating them nearly every day, perfectly content and trim.

SALAD PART 3. THE PROTEIN ON TOP

You may have guessed from some of my recipes and videos that I am not a "measurer" or "macro counter." When people ask, "How much protein do you eat?" I stumble around searching for an actual answer because my brain just wants to blurt out, "I eat whatever I feel like." My protein intake does vary, and I make no effort at all to measure it or to eat in a certain framework of macro intake that is common in the world of ketogenic diets. However, all of my salads do include a decent amount of protein. When using the "size of a deck of cards" measurement, I typically eat about two decks, about 6 ounces (180 grams), leaning toward 8 ounces (225 grams).

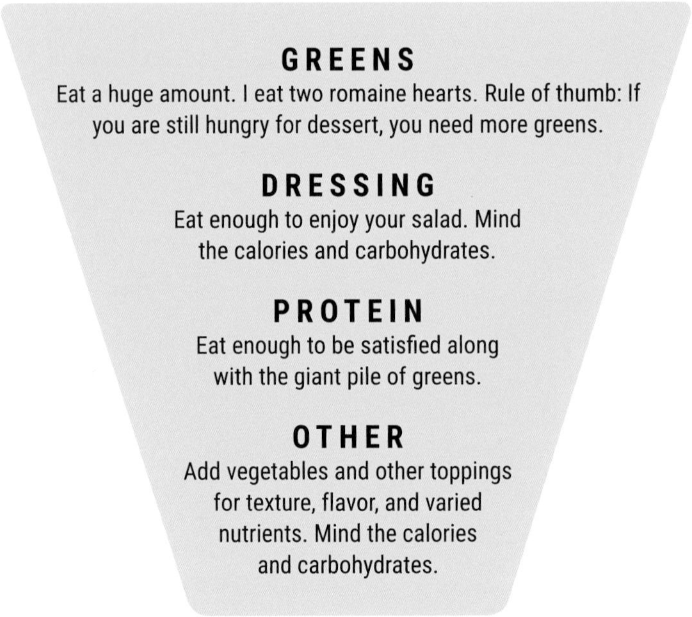

GREENS

Eat a huge amount. I eat two romaine hearts. Rule of thumb: If you are still hungry for dessert, you need more greens.

DRESSING

Eat enough to enjoy your salad. Mind the calories and carbohydrates.

PROTEIN

Eat enough to be satisfied along with the giant pile of greens.

OTHER

Add vegetables and other toppings for texture, flavor, and varied nutrients. Mind the calories and carbohydrates.

FIGURE 4: The parts of the RBS

As you eat your salads, you will probably figure out about how much protein you need to feel satisfied. In the keto world, some experts get concerned that we will eat too much protein. I am not sure where the research will land on this one, and I do not really worry about it because the huge amount of salad greens you have under your protein really does limit your protein intake. If you eat all of the greens, you simply will not have room in your stomach for a huge amount of protein. That said, on days when I seem to be craving protein, I eat more. I cannot imagine that a protein craving is a bad craving, and so I go with it. Eggs are a particularly good tool for these sorts of days; they are loaded with protein and minimal in calories. Eggs go well on or next to many salads.

SALAD PART 4. THE OTHER STUFF

Your Ridiculously Big Salad has greens, homemade dressing, and a whole-foods protein. To make the salad complete in terms of flavor and texture, you will likely add other items to your salad. However, be mindful of what you are adding, particularly if you have a lot of weight to lose. These are very big salads, and you can easily overload a salad with something like this selection of healthy, low-carb foods: ½ cup (120 ml) sunflower seeds, 1 avocado, and ½ cup (120 ml) feta cheese. With those quantities, completely possible and delicious on a salad of this size, the added calories would be in the range of 900 calories: 400 for the seeds, 300 for the avocado, and 200 for the feta. If you kept the add-ons in the range of 300 calories instead of 900, you would lose an extra estimated 5 or 6 pounds (2.2 to 2.7 kg) in a month, compared to a month in which you might pile on all three items. For people who join our community with a weight loss plateau, overeating calories is often the cause.

In the case of these salad toppings, they are all great foods and make all of the keto-friendly food lists, but too much of a good thing keeps you from burning your body fat. In my period of intensive weight loss, I tended to add one of these items instead of all three at once, or perhaps I would add two, but in more moderate quantities.

Speaking of keto-friendly foods, as you add toppings to your salads, eat some items on the side, or take a day off here or there from the salad. You will have best results if you keep your choices very low in carbohydrates and stay mindful of the calories. If you are new to learning about the carbohydrates and calories in foods, a food app might be in order, to help you get started. My cheat sheet in figure 5 may help as well.

THE CARBOHYDRATES IN THE RIDICULOUSLY BIG SALAD

With the popularity of ketogenic diets, I get many questions about how I count the macronutrients in my food and, more specifically, whether I count net carbs or total carbs, and how many carbs are allowed. Total carbohydrates are easily identified on a food label as "carbohydrates." The "net carbs" in your food are the total carbohydrates minus the fiber. Fiber is a carbohydrate that does not digest like sugars and starches, with added benefits as well. Many people subtract out these carbohydrates, as I do in the featured recipes in this book.

EAT BEARISHLY: leafy greens; unprocessed meat, fish, and seafood; eggs; non-root vegetables; coffee; tea; stevia and monk fruit (sweeteners); oils (olive, coconut, avocado).

EAT WITH RESTRAINT: processed meat (read labels), dairy (cheese, yogurt, sour cream, etc.: read labels), nuts and seeds, berries, condiments (read labels or make your own), root vegetables, beans and legumes, whole grains (read labels).

DO NOT EAT: sugared drinks, juice, coffee "creamer," alcohol, white flour products (e.g., bread, pasta, crackers, pretzels), potatoes and related products (e.g., chips, fries), breakfast cereal.

WHEN TO EAT: reduce your eating window. Give your body's hormones a rest. I eat in 1 hour each day. Keep your eating in 8 hours or less. Eat in 5 hours (or 1 hour!) for better results.

SNACKS: CUT THEM OUT. If you're eating in a larger window (5–8 hours), try eating two distinct meals and cutting out the snacks in between. Even a snack will affect your insulin level.

FIGURE 5: My "Getting Started" Cheat Sheet. You may only need to cut out the biggest offenders in red. You may need to be more intensive. Stick to the Green Zone.

My way of thinking on this topic is perhaps not quite as simple and may not be particularly satisfying to people coming from various branches of the ketogenic diet community. However, I have no doubt that we can still be friends. My view comes from my mind-set during my intensive weight-loss phase, in those eight months in which I lost 100 pounds (45 kilograms). Bear with me through another story, as I describe my philosophy on the carbohydrate content of my salads.

Consider first that I began this particular diet completely jaded about weight loss programs, and I was gearing up for bariatric surgery, planned for four months later. With surgery in my future, I was completely closed off to any other weight-loss messages.

I have many friends in the natural health and ketogenic diet worlds, all of whom would have helped me in this difficult time, had I asked for help. I shut out all those sources of information because I had already made the decision to give up and have the surgery. I was no longer engaged on the topic. I was going to lose some more weight before the surgery and practice more of the daily discipline that I knew I needed to master so that the bariatric surgery would be successful. I was highly committed to succeeding. I simply wanted to walk without limping, and I would fight for it.

If I was not going to speak to my own friends about my situation, the last thing I would have done was to read a bunch of internet content on the ketogenic diet. As I look back, I suspect my avoidance of confusing and disparate sources of information on the keto diet was a big success factor for me.

As I laid on that couch on a water fast, contemplating what I would be eating after the fast, I had a great deal of background knowledge on food, and I had tried many diets. The most successful diets for me up to that point were ones low in carbohydrates. However, those low-carb diets never quite hit the mark. I struggled a great deal with hunger, and I would get bored very quickly of meat, eggs, and cheese (along with the three little broccoli florets I would allow myself). I was about to try the one-meal-a-day model for the first time, because of the scuttlebutt that the framework helped with weight loss. I did not believe it would help at all, but I had four months before bariatric surgery and thought I would give it a try. I did no internet reading on it and performed no searches of PubMed or Google Scholar.

There is some common advice out there I did not see until I had lost the weight. I might have found the suggestion to transition to one meal a day over a six-month period because otherwise it is just too difficult to implement. I might have read that I must follow a ketogenic diet for months beforehand, otherwise it is just too difficult to implement. I might have been convinced that I needed to eat a mountain of fat to be satisfied with my meals, and I might have loaded up on the calories. Had I found all of this information and complicated my implementation, I probably would have ended up getting bariatric surgery.

Likewise, on the salad concept itself, in those early days isolated on my couch, I did not look up the carbohydrates in lettuce, nor the philosophy of lettuce in ketogenic circles. Had I done so, I might have become overly concerned that one head of iceberg lettuce has a whopping 22 grams of carbohydrates and 9 grams of dietary fiber, leaving it with 13 net grams of carbohydrates, a high amount when your daily limit is 20 net grams (a common limit in the world of keto diets). In fact, an Eat Like a Bear! community member popped one of my salads into the app "Carb Manager," and the salad received a grade of F. Apparently, I flunked my way right out of bariatric surgery. Had it been my intention to do a "proper" keto diet, and had I used app-powered algorithms to make my plans, I would have never considered the salad approach.

As it was, on previous low-carb diets I kept my vegetable intake very low, and those diets did not work for me. In this seemingly thousandth iteration of dieting, as I laid on the couch, considering what I would eat to break my water fast, I knew three things:

1. I would eat one meal a day because, what the heck, I had not tried that before.
2. My biggest barrier to a successful diet seemed to be hunger. I had struggled so much with hunger on previous diets, and the idea of one meal a day seemed impossible to implement, but I would try it anyway. In light of this, if I would eat only once, I would eat big.
3 My meal would include a lot of greens because, with just one meal, I was going to make it count and eat a giant meal, perhaps stretching out my stomach one final time before it would be reduced to 10 percent of its former size by my bariatric surgeon.

I was trying something out of desperation, an eating framework I would have never implemented had I paid attention to many of the popular recommendations. I had nothing to lose at that point and was not concerned about the opinions of my friends in natural health circles nor about the larger dieting community. Bariatric surgery was my ace in the hole, and this particular iteration of dieting was my practice in discipline, one last time before my surgeon would give me a new tool.

From this mind-set emerged the Ridiculously Big Salad, a way of eating that, frankly, has become somewhat legendary among those same natural health friends whom I avoided at that time. I do many things in the extreme, and it amuses me to look back on the origin of the Ridiculously Big Salad, a framework born in these very specific circumstances. I shut out the noise of the internet and gave it all one last go, going big, as I counted the weeks to surgery. In the words of my surgeon's physician's assistant, *"Aren't you glad you were approved for bariatric surgery?"*

As it was, for as quickly as it worked and as effective as it was, I was in such a pre-surgery mindset that it took me weeks of success to realize I would not need the surgery at all. By Week 2 of the Ridiculously Big Salad, I should have known things were different this time, but I had no expectation that this approach would work. It would be weeks later, on that day in November that I describe in the prologue, when my mind-set would change.

That long story is all background to these often-asked questions: *How do I count the carbohydrates in my salad? Will the 22 grams of carbohydrates in a head of iceberg lettuce make me fat?* These are the exact questions I would have asked had I actually used a ketogenic diet framework to create my meal plan back on that couch in 2017.

By now you might guess my answers: I do not count the carbohydrates in salad greens *at all*. The carbohydrate content of iceberg lettuce is not actually very high; it just appears high to those of us with more extreme mind-sets. In the early days of the diet, I used the cheap urine test strips for ketones to see if my body was producing them. It was. I was losing weight like I never had before, and, shockingly, I was far less hungry than I had ever been. I kept eating the salad, unconcerned about the optics in the keto community. Optics matter very little when you can end up half your size, well below the bariatric surgery projections, with your stomach completely intact.

As for measuring salads, I do not worry about the lettuce for the most part; however, I am highly mindful of the carbohydrates and calories in the rest of the salad. That said, in the featured salads in this book, I do include the carbohydrates in the greens in the data I provide. Because the greens are included, most salads end up in the range of 20 to 30 net grams of carbohydrates. Most ketogenic sources recommend eating under 20 grams of net carbs a day. If you follow those frameworks, you can easily adapt any of these recipes to hit the 20-gram net mark just by cutting out a vegetable or two. Everyone needs to find a framework that works for her or him.

For those of you navigating the keto diet world right now, here is my key recommendation: Replicate what I did for two weeks. Unless you have some complicated health condition, the best data you can collect will not come from a keto website or an app on your smartphone; it will come from your own two-week implementation of what I describe in this book. If an app helps you implement it, use it by all means. If it keeps you from getting started, delete it right now.

As I say in the prologue, if you look around and see a pit of fire, you have all you need to succeed. Start eating the Ridiculously Big Salad as if your life depends on it. The Ridiculously Big Salad works for many reasons, but a core reason in the context of counting macronutrients is this: It is simple. You do not need to count. You can focus all of that counting energy instead on being awesome. Go be awesome.

If you are *ravenously* seeking dessert after your Ridiculously Big Salad, your salad needs to be *ridiculously* bigger.

PICKLED EGGS: PORTABLE SALAD FLAVOR

I eat a lot of eggs these days on these salads, and pickled eggs just offer a fun variation on flavor, in a kitchen-crafty way. Pickling eggs allows you to infuse any flavor you like right into the boiled egg. Use any edible flavoring agent in the universe. There is no limit, and your egg becomes a portable little flavor nugget. Consider a mustard-infused boiled egg. It tastes a lot like a deviled egg.

I take pickled eggs on the road when I want some interesting flavors and protein on my salad. Imagine a romaine-based salad with a basic oil-and-vinegar dressing, boiled eggs, red onions, and pine nuts under towering conifer trees in a campground.

The flavor you infuse into your egg is completely up to you. However, my top choices are mustard, garlic, basil, thyme, and cilantro. Here are some principles to live by:

- If you let your eggs infuse in your refrigerator for a week (or however long), and the flavor is not yet strong, give them a few more days.

- Use a medium-size egg for this project. A smaller egg needs less time for the flavor to reach deep into the yolk.

- In many cases, you will be most successful if you use the dried or powdered form of the herb or spice because it will more readily infuse into the egg.

- If you use pickling spices, the spices are typically heated in the vinegar solution. That helps release the flavors of the whole spices. If your spices are ground, this step is less necessary, but it is good to note that heating the spices will always help you get more flavor out of them. It is not a bad idea.

The Process

1. Boil the eggs. Allow them to cool. Peel them.

2. Layer your eggs and herbs and spices into a quart (liter) jar. A dozen medium-size eggs will actually fit in one jar.

3. As for quantities of herbs, I use about a fist-full of fresh herbs in a quart (liter) jar of eggs. If it is a dry herb, I might use a tablespoon (15 ml). I might add 3–5 garlic cloves.

4. Fill your jar halfway with apple cider vinegar. Top with water. Secure with a plastic lid.

5. Give the mixture a good swish, and place it in your refrigerator for at least a few days (for smaller eggs) or a week for better flavor. They may last longer, but plan to eat them within a month.

chapter four

Homemade Salad Dressings

A critical component to the Ridiculously Big Salad is the dressing. Most diet salads severely limit the calories and fat in the dressing portion of the salad. The fifteen salad dressing recipes you find here, however, are a big source of your daily calories and fat. The fat in these dressings will help you feel more satisfied with the meal and will help carry more of the flavor throughout the salad. Many of the dressings also include apple cider vinegar, an ingredient that may help you feel full sooner. If you are eating a salad without apple cider vinegar in it, consider having an ounce or so (30 ml), diluted in a few ounces (90 ml) of water as you prepare your salad for the day. Try it and see if it brings you to fullness more quickly. It works very well for me.

As for the recipes in this section, I have tried to keep them as simple as possible to give you a starting place. All of them can be stepped up in some way. Infuse vinegars with your favorite flavors. Add dozens of other flavors to the vinaigrette and ranch dressings. Add gourmet vinegars. With anything you add, simply check the carbohydrates and calories. Otherwise, have a lot of fun experimenting. Your best salads will come out of this process.

If any of the recipe ingredients are new to you, peruse the ingredients list at the end of the book for descriptions and shopping tips.

CLASSIC VINAIGRETTE

You do not get more simple than this one. You can mix it up in a bowl or jar, as I describe here, or you can simply make it right on the greens by pouring and sprinkling each item onto the greens in your salad bowl. If you take the "toss it on the salad" approach, start with the oil and toss the leaves well to coat them. Add the vinegar, salt, and pepper next, and toss again. It is that simple. The portion below is plenty for one big salad, at nearly 490 calories and 0 grams of carbohydrates.

Classic Vinaigrette Ingredients (1 Salad)

¼ cup (60 ml) extra-virgin olive oil

¼ cup (60 ml) apple cider vinegar

¼ teaspoon (1 ml) salt

¼ teaspoon (1 ml) pepper

Classic Vinaigrette Steps

1. Add all ingredients to a measuring cup or bowl.
2. Combine.

DIJON VINAIGRETTE

This is just a variation of a classic vinaigrette dressing, with a bit of Dijon mustard and oregano. I do like to make this in a bowl or jar to ensure that the mustard and oregano are well distributed. You can ensure that they are well emulsified by adding the oil slowly to the vinegar and whisking vigorously as you drizzle on the oil. However, for a single-serving salad dressing, I never seem to bother. This recipe makes enough dressing for one big salad, at about 490 calories and 0 grams of carbohydrates.

Dijon Vinaigrette Ingredients (1 Salad)

¼ cup (60 ml) extra-virgin olive oil

¼ cup (60 ml) apple cider vinegar

1 teaspoon (5 ml) Dijon mustard

¼ teaspoon (1 ml) dried oregano

ingredients continued on page 62

classic vinaigrette

dijon vinaigrette

¼ teaspoon (1 ml) salt

¼ teaspoon (1 ml) pepper

Dijon Vinaigrette Steps

1. Add all ingredients to a measuring cup or bowl.

2. Combine.

RANCH DRESSING

This one is so simple that I make it on an on-demand basis and rarely keep it stored in the refrigerator. Of course, on the occasion in which I do have extra and have it stored, I always seem to find uses for it and am happy to have it. As with all of these little kitchen projects, go either way. The recipe below is approximately what I use for one big salad. Multiply it to your heart's content. This quantity is about 500 calories and 2 grams of carbohydrates. With all recipes, check the labels on your ingredients, especially for added sugar.

Ranch Dressing Ingredients (1 Salad)

¼ cup (60 ml) mayonnaise

¼ cup (60 ml) Greek yogurt or sour cream

2 teaspoons (10 ml) chopped parsley (or ½ teaspoon, 2 ml, dried)

2 teaspoons (10 ml) chopped chives (or ½ teaspoon, 2 ml, dried)

2 teaspoons (10 ml) chopped dill weed (or ½ teaspoon, 2 ml, dried)

Water to reach desired consistency

Salt and pepper, to taste

Ranch Dressing Steps

1. In a bowl, combine mayonnaise and Greek yogurt or sour cream.

2. Add herbs. Combine.

3. Adjust consistency with water.

4. Add salt and pepper.

ranch dressing

COLESLAW DRESSING

I make this dressing on demand a couple of times a week. It is probably my favorite in the world of "solid, workhorse performers." I use it primarily on cabbage and broccoli slaw, but it goes well on any sort of green. The recipe below is approximately what I use for one big salad. Double or triple it. Quintuple it! This quantity is about 500 calories and under 1 gram of carbohydrates. With all recipes, however, check the ingredients for added sugar.

Coleslaw Dressing Ingredients (1 Salad)

¼ cup (60 ml) mayonnaise

¼ cup (60 ml) Greek yogurt or sour cream

1 tablespoon (15 ml) apple cider vinegar

Sweeten to taste with stevia, monk fruit, or other sugar-free sweetener of choice

Salt and pepper, to taste

Water to reach desired consistency

Coleslaw Dressing Steps

1. In a bowl, combine mayonnaise and Greek yogurt or sour cream.
2. Add apple cider vinegar, stevia, and a dash of salt and pepper.
3. Adjust consistency with water.
4. Taste and adjust for sweetness, salt, and pepper. (Adjust your final salad, too.)

CAESAR DRESSING

When I make this dressing, I make enough for two salads because, frankly, I have to dirty a blender or food processor to make it. Any time heavy equipment gets involved in a recipe, I double it at least. The recipe below is approximately what I use for two salads. If you use this quantity for two salads, your calories are at 475 with about 8 grams of carbohydrates per salad. The carbohydrates are in the yogurt, parmesan cheese, lemon juice, and garlic powder. With all recipes, however, check the labels on your specific ingredients, especially for any added sugar.

coleslaw dressing

Caesar Dressing Ingredients (2 Salads)

¼ cup (60 ml) extra virgin olive oil

¼ cup (60 ml) lemon juice

1 cup (240 ml) Greek yogurt

⅔ cup (160 ml) grated Parmesan cheese

2 teaspoons (10 ml) anchovy paste

2 teaspoons (10 ml) Dijon mustard

⅔ teaspoon (3 ml) garlic powder

Water to reach desired consistency

Salt and pepper, to taste

Caesar Dressing Steps

1. In a blender or food processor, add olive oil, lemon juice, Greek yogurt, Parmesan cheese, anchovy paste, Dijon mustard, and garlic powder. Blend until smooth.

2. Adjust consistency with water.

3. Taste and adjust for salt and pepper.

caesar dressing

italian dressing

ITALIAN DRESSING (AND CREAMY ITALIAN)

This is a great classic dressing that you may use quite a bit as you experiment with your salads. This is a 500-calorie dressing with 0 grams of carbohydrates. If you are missing some of these herbs, you will still end up with a good dressing.

Italian Dressing Ingredients (1 Salad)

¼ cup (60 ml) avocado oil

¼ cup (60 ml) apple cider vinegar

1 teaspoon (5 ml) Dijon mustard

1 teaspoon (5 ml) each dried basil, oregano, and parsley

¼ teaspoon (1 ml) each dried thyme, sage, and rosemary

¼ teaspoon (1 ml) each garlic powder and onion powder

¼ teaspoon (1 ml) each salt and pepper

poppy seed dressing

Italian Dressing Steps

1. Combine all ingredients in a bowl or jar.

2. Mix well. Adjust for salt and pepper to taste. If dried spices are older, allow the dressing to sit for an hour or so (or at least for 10 minutes) for the flavors to infuse into the oil and vinegar.

For the Creamy Italian variation, replace the avocado oil and apple cider vinegar with 3 tablespoons (50 ml) avocado oil, 3 tablespoons (50 ml) apple cider vinegar, and 3 tablespoons (50 ml) Greek yogurt. Add water, if needed to reach desired consistency.

POPPY SEED DRESSING

This poppy seed dressing is a simple and delicious staple, waiting for you to whip it up. The recipe may take an entire three minutes to make, with one-third of that time tied up in gathering the ingredients. The recipe below is approximately what I use for one salad. Scale it up for more. This quantity is 580 calories and 4 grams of carbohydrates (3 net), with the carbs primarily in the yogurt and poppy seeds. With all recipes, however, check the labels on your ingredients for added sugar.

Poppy Seed Dressing Ingredients (1 Salad)

3 tablespoons (50 ml) mayonnaise

¼ cup (60 ml) Greek yogurt

1 tablespoon (15 ml) extra-virgin olive oil

1 tablespoon (15 ml) apple cider vinegar

Sugar-free sweetener (stevia, monk fruit, or another of your choice)

1 tablespoon (15 ml) poppy seeds

¼ teaspoon (1 ml) salt

Water to reach desired consistency

Poppy Seed Dressing Steps

1. In a bowl, combine all ingredients, and blend well.

2. Adjust consistency with water.

3. Adjust for sweetener and salt.

"HONEY" MUSTARD DRESSING

This one does not actually contain honey, but it is a sweet mustard dressing that certainly does the job. Many variations of this classic use all oil or mayonnaise, but I use half Greek yogurt just to shave off some calories, as I do with many of these dressings. If you do not have mustard powder, you can use prepared yellow mustard. The recipe below is approximately what I use for one salad. Scale it up and go bananas. This quantity is 460 calories and 5 grams of carbohydrates (4 net). With all recipes, however, check the labels on your ingredients, especially for added sugar.

"Honey" Mustard Dressing Ingredients (1 Salad)

¼ cup (60 ml) mayonnaise

¼ cup (60 ml) Greek yogurt

½ tablespoon (6 ml) mustard powder

½ tablespoon (6 ml) Dijon mustard

1 tablespoon (15 ml) apple cider vinegar

½ tablespoon (6 ml) lemon juice

Water to reach desired consistency

Sugar-free sweetener (stevia, monk fruit, or another of your choice)

Salt and pepper, to taste

"Honey" Mustard Dressing Steps

1. In a bowl, combine all ingredients, and blend well.

2. Adjust consistency with water.

3. Adjust for sweetener, salt, and pepper.

"honey" mustard dressing

ASIAN PEANUT DRESSING

This is a super-simple dressing that's loaded with peanut flavor and great over cabbage, a spring mix, iceberg, or romaine. It pairs well with most of the protein toppers, notably chicken, pork, and shrimp. Make a single batch for a single big salad or double or triple it. This one brings about 500 calories for the portion below and about 9 grams of carbohydrates (7 net).

Asian Peanut Dressing Ingredients (1 Salad)

3 tablespoons (50 ml) avocado oil

2 tablespoons (30 ml) apple cider vinegar

3 tablespoons (50 ml) peanut powder (or peanut butter)

½ tablespoon (6 ml) sesame oil

2 tablespoons (30 ml) soy sauce or tamari

¼ teaspoon (1 ml) ginger powder

¼ teaspoon (1 ml) garlic powder

Sugar-free sweetener (stevia, monk fruit, or another of your choice)

Salt and pepper, to taste

Asian Peanut Dressing Steps

1. In a bowl, combine all ingredients, and blend well.
2. Adjust for sweetener, salt, and pepper.

asian peanut dressing

ASIAN TERIYAKI VINAIGRETTE DRESSING

This is a great, hard-working dressing with a lot of flavor. It is excellent over lettuce or cabbage, making it highly versatile. It comes in at 300 calories and 5 grams of carbohydrates.

Asian Vinaigrette Dressing Ingredients (1 Salad)

3 tablespoons (50 ml) soy sauce or tamari

¼ cup (60 ml) apple cider vinegar

2 tablespoons (30 ml) avocado oil

½ teaspoon (2 ml) ginger powder

½ teaspoon (2 ml) garlic powder

½ teaspoon (2 ml) pepper

Sugar-free sweetener (stevia, monk fruit, or another of your choice)

Salt, to taste

Asian Vinaigrette Dressing Steps

1. In a bowl, combine all ingredients.
2. Adjust for sweetener, salt, and pepper.

asian teriyaki vinaigrette dressing

tartar sauce dressing

TARTAR SAUCE DRESSING

This tartar sauce dressing is inspired by the classic tartar sauce you would find on the coast next to a basket of fish and chips. Pair it with fish on your salad. This portion is for one Ridiculously Big Salad, but make as much as you wish. This dressing hits the 430-calorie mark, and the carbohydrates are in the yogurt and pickles, probably in the 3 to 6 range.

Tartar Sauce Dressing Ingredients (1 Salad)

¼ cup (60 ml) mayonnaise

¼ cup (60 ml) Greek yogurt

1 dill pickle spear, diced

3 tablespoons (45 ml) dill pickle juice

1 tablespoon (15 ml) fresh lemon juice

Water to reach desired consistency

¼ teaspoon (1 ml) pepper

¼ teaspoon (1 ml) salt

Tartar Sauce Dressing Steps

1. In a bowl, combine all ingredients, and blend well.

2. Adjust consistency with water.

3. Adjust for salt and pepper.

BLUE CHEESE DRESSING

This basic blue cheese dressing could be loaded with even more blue cheese, if you want a super-cheesy salad. The recipe below is for a double batch, to make two separate salads. Whereas most salad dressings I make on demand, one salad at a time, this one I double because the measuring is just easier and the crumbling of the cheese makes this feel like a more difficult dressing. I put half in a jar for later, but plan to eat that half within the next week. It will last longer than that, but I do not have a lot of extra room in the refrigerator, and it is easy for small items like this to get lost and spoil. Half of the recipe below (for one salad), comes in at about 500 calories and 2 grams of carbohydrates.

In regard to the blue cheese, you get what you pay for. As a simple measure of quality, look for the blue cheese you crumble or slice into cubes yourself, rather than one crumbled for you.

Blue Cheese Dressing Ingredients (2 Salads)

½ cup (120 ml) crumbled blue cheese

¼ cup (60 ml) mayonnaise

¼ cup (60 ml) Greek yogurt plus 2 tablespoons (30 ml) whey

¼ cup (60 ml) apple cider vinegar

3 tablespoons (45 ml) extra-virgin olive oil

Water to reach desired consistency

Sugar-free sweetener (stevia, monk fruit, or another of your choice)

¼ teaspoon (1 ml) pepper

¼ teaspoon (1 ml) salt

Blue Cheese Dressing Steps

1. In a bowl, combine all ingredients.

2. Adjust consistency with water.

3. Adjust for sweetener, salt, and pepper.

blue cheese dressing

CHEESEBURGER DRESSING

This is the dressing for the ever-popular cheeseburger salad, which is simply this dressing over iceberg lettuce, the ground beef protein topper, dill pickles, grated cheddar cheese, and optional onions. The recipe below is for a double batch because you will have it twice in Week 3. You may want to double it again if you have someone with whom to share it. This dressing recipe comes in at about 450 calories and 3 grams of carbohydrates.

Cheeseburger Dressing Ingredients (2 Salads)

½ cup (120 ml) mayonnaise

½ cup (120 ml) Greek yogurt

¼ cup (60 ml) chopped dill pickle

1½ teaspoons (7 ml) prepared yellow mustard

1 teaspoon (5 ml) apple cider vinegar

Water to reach desired consistency

½ teaspoon (2 ml) paprika

¼ teaspoon (1 ml) garlic powder

¼ teaspoon (1 ml) onion powder

Sugar-free sweetener (stevia, monk fruit, or another of your choice)

Salt and pepper, to taste

Cheeseburger Dressing Steps

1. In a bowl, combine all ingredients.
2. Adjust for sweetness, salt, and pepper.

cheeseburger dressing

CILANTRO VINAIGRETTE

This simple dressing is a variation of a salsa we found in a Colombian recipe years ago. I have made it with all vinegar, and it is delicious. You could easily cut the oil or reduce the oil by half and still have a great dressing, if you want to shave a few calories off this salad. The recipe below makes a double batch for two big salads. I make two portions at a time, mainly because I get my blender dirty. With that level of commitment, I make enough for two salads. You could make even more if you wish. For one salad you can expect about 500 calories and 1 gram of carbohydrates.

Cilantro Vinaigrette Ingredients (2 Salads)

½ cup (120 ml) avocado oil

½ cup (120 ml) apple cider vinegar

2 cups (480 ml) packed fresh cilantro (cut main stems off, discard) — about two "bunches" worth

2 cloves fresh garlic, chopped

½ teaspoon (2 ml) pepper

½ teaspoon (2 ml) salt

Cilantro Vinaigrette Steps

1. Put all ingredients in a blender or food processor.
2. Pulse until the cilantro is well integrated.

cilantro dressing

GREEN GODDESS DRESSING

There are so many variations of this dressing. If you cannot find one of these herbs or do not like one, you can simply omit it or replace it. Do not let the anchovy paste in this one scare you. Like the Caesar Dressing, it simply adds a savory flavor. It will not make the dressing "fishy." This one totals 530 calories and about 3.5 grams of carbohydrates.

Green Goddess Dressing Ingredients (2 Salads)

½ cup (120 ml) extra-virgin olive oil
½ cup (120 ml) plain Greek yogurt
½ cup (120 ml) loosely packed fresh parsley
¼ cup (60 ml) loosely packed fresh chives
¼ cup (60 ml) loosely packed fresh tarragon
2 teaspoons (10 ml) anchovy paste
1 clove garlic, chopped
1 teaspoon (5 ml) salt

Green Goddess Dressing Steps

1. Blend ingredients together in a blender.
2. Adjust for salt.

Note: After tasting, if the herbal flavor of the dressing is too strong, you can dilute it with some more oil and/or yogurt.

green goddess dressing

The Ridiculously Big Salad works for many reasons, but a core reason in the context of counting macronutrients is this: It is *simple*. You do not need to count. You can focus all of that counting energy instead on being *awesome*. Go be awesome.

chapter five

Batch-Cooked Protein Toppers

Much of the protein you are going to add to your salads in the next six weeks you will cook yourself in larger batches. Some protein will come out of a can or a bag, just to give you a little break. All of the protein items you cook will be very basic in both how they are cooked and the seasoning that you use. Keeping the cooking method simple, of course, keeps everything simple, and that is never a bad thing. Keeping the seasonings basic not only simplifies the cooking but also allows you flexibility in the eventual salad that you make.

As you will see, my approach is to season the meats with a light touch and to bring the distinctive flavor to the salad via the salad dressing. This allows you to pull chicken out of your freezer and add it to a Cobb Salad, an Asian Teriyaki Salad, or to shred it and make a simple chicken salad to pack for the road and pop on top of your romaine and vinaigrette. In each of these recipes, I use Old Bay Seasoning to season the meats. It is available basically everywhere and has no carbohydrates. If you cannot find it or do not like it, just season your meat with salt, pepper, garlic powder, and onion powder. Keep it simple.

EQUIPMENT

- **Pressure Cooker.** You do not need one, but these recipes are just so much easier with a pressure cooker like an Instant Pot. I have oven or stovetop recipes here for all of these protein items, but you will save time and fuss with this device.
- **Digital Meat Thermometer.** It is a good thing to check your meat for doneness, just to make sure you are meeting food safety standards.
- **Slow Cooker (Crock-Pot).** If you do not have a pressure cooker, a slow cooker is another option. I provide instructions for

using a slow cooker, as relevant, although increasingly I gravitate to the pressure cooker in my own kitchen.

On the following pages there are instructions for cooking the various meats that you will find in your six-week salad plan. If you have a different favorite way to cook these meats, by all means use your method.

CHICKEN BREASTS

Chicken breasts are extremely convenient to have for salads, but they tend to be quite expensive if you buy them already cooked. I recommend that you buy them frozen and prepare them in larger batches using one of these simple methods. I tend to buy 3 to 4 pounds (1.5–2 kg) at a time and cook them in my pressure cooker. From one batch I ended up feeding myself and my family some sort of chicken-based meal and then froze at least four baggies of chicken for future salads. You can find frozen boneless, skinless chicken breasts at just about any store you frequent. Buy gourmet quality if you can afford it; shop by price if things are tight.

COOK IT IN THE PRESSURE COOKER
My favorite method for cooking frozen boneless, skinless chicken breasts is the pressure cooker, an Instant Pot in my case. It simply does not get easier.

1. **Season the chicken.** Using frozen chicken breasts (3–4 pounds, 1.5–2 kg), sprinkle on Old Bay Seasoning, giving them a good dusting (about ¼ teaspoon [1 ml] per breast if you are measuring — a light dusting if you are not). Place the breasts in the pressure cooker.
2. **Moisten.** Add 1 cup (240 ml) of broth or water to the pressure cooker.
3. **Seal.** Close and seal the pressure cooker. Check the vent to make sure it is set to "seal."

CHICKEN
inspiration

CHICKEN CAESAR SALAD, FROM WEEK 3

This is a simple classic salad, satisfying and filling. One serving of the Caesar Salad Dressing in the recipe section of this book makes this salad rich and delicious. A traditional Caesar includes croutons. If you are looking for that little extra crunch and flavor, I recommend adding the "cheese crisp" products you can find near the produce and salad section of the grocery store. They are crunchy little nuggets of cheese that pair well in flavor and texture with this traditional recipe. You can also make your own cheese crisps with Parmesan cheese by baking little mounds of grated Parmesan in your oven at about 400°F (200°C) for 4 minutes. Altogether this recipe comes in at about 1,000 calories and 14 net grams of carbohydrates (6 net grams from the lettuce) without the cheese crisp option.

INGREDIENTS
- 2 hearts of romaine, chopped
- ½ cup (120 ml) grated Parmesan cheese
- 6 ounces (180 g) chicken strips
- 1 serving of Caesar Salad Dressing
- Optional: "cheese crisps"

4. **Cook**. Set on manual for 10 minutes if frozen, 6 minutes if fresh. If the breasts are extra-large, add about 2 minutes. (Breasts are usually in the 6–8 ounce range, about 200 grams. You can check yours by checking the weight on the package, counting the breasts, and dividing to get an average.) If you have any doubt as to cooking time, a meat thermometer is a great tool for a quick check. Chicken should reach 165°F (74°C) for doneness and food safety.

5. **Release**. Allow the pressure cooker to release the steam naturally for about five minutes, and then release it if need be.

6. **Cool**. Remove the chicken from the pot to cool it more quickly and to keep it from overcooking.

COOK IT IN THE OVEN

1. **Preheat**. Preheat the oven to 425°F (220°C). Place a baking rack in the middle of the oven.

2. **Oil and season**. Rub avocado oil on the frozen chicken breasts. Sprinkle on Old Bay Seasoning, giving them a good dusting (about ¼ teaspoon [1 ml] per breast if you are measuring — a light dusting if you are not). Place the breasts on a baking sheet lined with parchment paper or a silicone sheet.

3. **Roast**. Roast the chicken, uncovered, for 30 to 40 minutes. Check for doneness beginning at 30 minutes, using a meat thermometer to check for an internal temperature of 165°F (74°C). A thorough food safety person would check in the thickest part of the breast and would test each breast, ensuring that they were all completely cooked.

4. **Cool**. When done, allow the chicken to cool before freezing.

5. **Freeze.**

FREEZING METHOD

When the chicken is cooked, I allow it to cool and then place it into freezer bags, in the approximate quantities I will be using. Sometimes I freeze enough for my own salad. Sometimes I freeze a quantity that I know my family will eat. It simply depends on how much I have, how limited my salad protein stash is, and how much my family seems to be into chicken at the moment.

I freeze the chicken in whole breast pieces and then typically cut them into strips or shred them on a salad-by-salad basis when I defrost them. I keep them whole simply because they are less likely to get freezer burn, and I have the flexibility to use them as I wish later.

Pack each baggie, but do not over pack them. Make sure you can flatten the baggie out a bit so that they will stack in your freezer. If you overstuff the baggie, it will end up in a puffy ball shape and will just roll around in your freezer.

DEFROSTING METHOD

Since you have packed your chicken in serving sizes useful to you, simply grab a baggie out of the freezer and put the contents into a covered skillet with a bit of water. Heat it on medium-low until defrosted, and warm (about 10 minutes). Cut the chicken into strips or shred it with a fork, whichever suits your salad.

GROUND BEEF, PORK, TURKEY, OR CHICKEN

Cooking ground meats is so ridiculously simple that you can easily make these staple items to fill your freezer. Watch for sales and load up your shopping cart. I tend to cook these meats about 3 to 5 pounds (1.5–2.4 kg) at a time, using two larger 18-inch (500-cm) skillets to do so.

COOK IT ON THE STOVETOP

1. **Heat the skillet**. Start heating the skillet on high.
2. **Add oil for lean meats**. If you are using a leaner meat, add a tablespoon (15 ml) or two of a high-heat oil (e.g., avocado oil) to the skillet.
3. **Cook**. Add ground meat to the hot skillet, using a spatula to break it up a bit. Continue to break it up as it cooks, about every 2 minutes. Cook for about 8 minutes.

GROUND BEEF
inspiration

TACO SALAD, FROM WEEK 2

Put all of your favorite taco flavors right into your salad. That really is the beauty of the taco: You can mix and match to create the perfect taco experience for yourself. For me, that perfect experience must have beef, cheddar cheese, white onion, avocado, cilantro, and tomato, as I include in this recipe. If you know me and my love of raw red onions, you might find white onion to be an odd choice. However, in Mexican cuisine white onion is mandatory. Not yellow onion. Not red. White. There is a certain spicy crispiness that just works, and I am certainly not going to second-guess the traditions of a culture that knows a whole lot about great flavor. The taco salad below totals about 1,200 calories and 17 net grams of carbohydrates (6 net grams from the lettuce).

INGREDIENTS

- 2 hearts of romaine lettuce, chopped
- 6 ounces (180 g) ground beef, cooked
- 1 medium tomato, sliced
- ¼ cup (60 ml) grated cheddar cheese
- ½ sliced white onion
- ½ avocado, sliced
- Cilantro for garnish
- 1 serving of Ranch Dressing

4. **Season**. Add about ½ tablespoon (6 ml) of Old Bay Seasoning per pound (480 g) of meat. Stir well. Adjust for salt and pepper.
5. **Cool**. Allow the meat to cool before storing in the freezer.
6. **Freeze**.

FREEZING METHOD

Place the ground meat into baggies in amounts appropriate for your salads. Zip the baggies closed, label, flatten, and stack in the freezer.

DEFROSTING METHOD

As needed, grab a baggie from the freezer for your salad. Put the contents of the baggie into a skillet on medium-low heat with a bit of water. Cover and heat until defrosted and warm, about 10 minutes.

BEEF OR PORK ROAST

You will cook your roast in a pressure cooker or a slow cooker. Using a frozen roast, the cook time for the pressure cooker will be just more than an hour. For the slow cooker, allow 9 hours.

The most common roast is a beef chuck roast, but follow the sales and use any roast. For pork, you will likely find pork loin, pork tenderloin, or pork shoulder. Some roasts will have bones to deal with, requiring you to cut the meat off them. In that case, use the bones for soup stock.

The roasts available in the market generally range from 2 to 7 pounds (1–3 kg). I do like to go big with all of these things, although a 5-pound (2.3 kg) roast is probably going to exceed the capacity of a smaller pressure cooker or slow cooker. Know the limits of your kitchen equipment to find the sweet spot.

COOK IT IN THE PRESSURE COOKER

1. **Season the meat**. Using the frozen roast, sprinkle on Old Bay Seasoning, giving it a good dusting (about 1 tablespoon per pound (30 ml per kg) if you are measuring, a light dusting if

you are not). Place the roast in the pressure cooker, on top of a trivet, particularly if the roast is frozen.

2. **Moisten.** Add 2 cups (480 ml) of broth or water to the pressure cooker. You can use any sort of bone broth you have, even if the bone type does not match the meat type you are cooking. It will simply add more flavor. Water works, too; it just does not have the additional flavor.

3. **Seal.** Close and seal the pressure cooker. Check the vent to make sure it is set to "seal."

4. **Cook.** Set on manual using these guidelines: 70 minutes for 2 pounds (1 kg) and 80 minutes for 3 pounds (1.4 kg). Add 10 minutes per additional pound (½ kg).

5. **Release.** When the timer beeps and the meat has been cooked, use the manual release option to release the steam and slow the additional cooking process.

6. **Cool.** Remove the meat from the pot to cool it more quickly. Slice the pork roast. Slice or shred the beef roast.

7. **Freeze.**

COOK IT IN THE SLOW COOKER

1. **Season the meat.** Using the frozen roast, sprinkle on Old Bay Seasoning, giving it a good dusting (about 1 tablespoon per pound [30 ml per kg] if you are measuring — a light dusting if you are not). Place the roast into the slow cooker.

2. **Moisten.** Add 2 cups (480 ml) of broth or water to the slow cooker.

3. **Cook.** Cook on low for 7 to 9 hours or on high for 5 to 6 hours. Check for doneness using a meat thermometer. It should reach an internal temperature of 145°F (63°C). (*Brands and models of slow cookers really do perform differently. Roast sizes vary. It is difficult, if not impossible, to provide a precise amount of cooking time. After your first time cooking a roast, make a note of your own process to help you next time.*)

4. **Cool.** Remove the roast from the pot to cool it more quickly. Slice it or shred it.

5. **Freeze.**

ROAST
inspiration

ASIAN TERIYAKI WITH PORK, FROM WEEK 3

This is a delicious, classic salad that can be deliciously lean if you so choose. As I was navigating my weight loss, I did have sets of days in which I purposefully shaved off some calories to try to make a little more progress. This salad, without the optional avocado, is just such an example. It is only about 650 calories, largely because of the leaner dressing. With the avocado it is 900 calories. The salad as written includes 23 net grams of carbohydrates (12 net grams from the spring mix).

INGREDIENTS

- 8 cups (2 liters) spring mix
- 6 ounces (180 g) pork roast
- 3 mini bell peppers, sliced
- 3 green onions, sliced
- Optional: 1 medium avocado, sliced
- 1 serving of Asian Teriyaki Dressing

FREEZING METHOD

Place pieces of roast into baggies in amounts appropriate for your salads. Zip the baggies closed, label, flatten, and stack in the freezer.

DEFROSTING METHOD

As needed, grab a baggie from the freezer for your salad. Put the contents of the baggie into a skillet on medium-low heat with a bit of water. Cover and heat until defrosted and warm (about 10 minutes).

BEEF STRIPS FROM STEAK

Beef strips are simple and delicious salad toppings. Here in California, I cook them as I would a carne asada, but I keep a light touch with the seasonings so that I am not stuck with the flavor of Mexican food on each of my salads. You can always add taco seasonings later. For this item find a basic cut like a flank steak, skirt steak, or a round steak cut as thin steaks. Sometimes you will find them already cut into strips, ready to cook. Either way works. Cook the strips much like you would ground beef, including stirring them every couple of minutes. They are extremely simple and quick to cook. Most people will be cooking the whole, thin steaks, so I provide those instructions to you here.

This recipe is so basic that I almost feel bad including it without a fancy marinade, but you will be adding a lot of flavor to your salad with your dressing, and this simple approach will allow you later to take these steak strips in any direction you wish. You could cook this in other ways, but it is really simple on the stovetop and is fairly quick as well. I recommend this approach (and we all have stovetops in our kitchens).

As with all meats, I would cook 3 to 5 pounds (1.5–2 kg). If you are working in a tiny kitchen with one skillet, you might keep it to 2 pounds (1 kg).

COOK IT ON THE STOVETOP

1. **Heat skillet(s).** Heat an extra-large skillet (or two) on high heat. Add about a tablespoon (15 ml) of avocado oil to each skillet.
2. **Cook.** When the skillet is hot, add the steak to the skillet in a single layer and sear for 3 minutes on each side.
3. **Rest.** Pull the meat off the heat and place it on a cutting board for 5 minutes.
4. **Continue.** Continue to cook other pieces of meat until you have cooked everything, 3 minutes on each side and 5 minutes to rest.
5. **Slice.** After resting for 5 minutes, slice it into thin, bite-size pieces, if it is not already sliced.

STEAK STRIP
inspiration

STEAK STRIPS WITH BLUE CHEESE DRESSING, FROM WEEK 4

Steak and blue cheese are fairly heavy and rich items, making this a great salad when you are feeling awfully hungry. However, it is easy to keep loading it with richness and going well over that ceiling of calories for which you are probably shooting. For this reason, I tend to put lighter items in the fourth part of the salad. In this case, I included tomato, bell pepper, and red onion, all quite low in calories and fairly low in carbohydrates. This salad comes in at 1,100 calories and about 21 net grams of carbohydrates (6 net grams from the romaine). If you want a salad lower still in carbohydrates, you can cut out the red onion and save about 6 grams, or eliminate the bell peppers to save about 4 grams.

INGREDIENTS

- 2 hearts of romaine, chopped
- 6 ounces (180 g) steak strips
- 1 medium tomato, sliced
- 3 mini bell peppers, sliced
- 1 small red onion, sliced
- 1 serving of Blue Cheese Dressing

BACON
inspiration

BACON, LETTUCE, AND TOMATO SALAD (OF COURSE), FROM WEEK 1

This salad appears in Week 1 of your six-week salad plan because I just do not think you should wait any longer to try this one. This is a simple salad that combines the classic flavors we all love. I add two eggs to this recipe because I find that when I am eating bacon, I can load up the calories if I am having no other substantial protein source. The eggs provide the extra protein with fewer calories. Eggs can serve this role on many salads, in fact. They have about 15 grams of protein and

about 150 calories, so two eggs added to a salad will add 30 grams of protein and only 300 calories to your daily intake. It is a pretty good strategy, depending on your needs. This recipe as written brings about 1,250 calories and 20 net grams of carbohydrates (13 net grams from the lettuce).

INGREDIENTS
- 1 head of iceberg lettuce, chopped
- 5 slices of bacon (or turkey bacon), crumbled
- 1 medium tomato, cubed
- 2 boiled eggs, sliced
- 1 serving of Ranch Dressing

FREEZING METHOD

Place steak strips in baggies in amounts appropriate for your salads. Zip the baggies closed, label, flatten, and stack in the freezer.

DEFROSTING METHOD

As needed, grab a baggie from the freezer for your salad. Put the contents of the baggie into a skillet on medium-low heat with a bit of water. Cover and heat until defrosted and warm (about 10 minutes).

BACON

Bacon is a great addition to salads, and it actually bakes well in the oven. It is a bit less messy to cook in the oven and a bit less fussy than in a skillet. I tend to cook 2 pounds (1 kg) at a time and do so when I have an hour or two of kitchen work. In my small old Wedgewood 1940s oven with one rack, I cook 2 pounds in about three batches, at about 25 minutes per batch. It is easy to cook. It is all a matter of minding the timer.

COOK IT IN THE OVEN

1. **Preheat.** Preheat your oven to 400°F (200°C).
2. **Line.** Line a baking sheet with foil, parchment paper, or a silicone liner for easier cleanup.
3. **Arrange.** Arrange the bacon on the baking sheet and bake to your desired crispness, 15 to 25 minutes.
4. **Cool.** Cool the first batch on a plate lined with a paper towel as you cook the second.
5. **Freeze.**

FREEZING METHOD

Place bacon into freezer baggies, in amounts appropriate for your salads. Zip the baggies closed, label, flatten, and stack in the freezer.

DEFROSTING METHOD

As needed, grab a baggie from the freezer for your salad. Leave it out for a few hours to defrost, or you can heat it in a skillet to use more immediately. Simply warm the bacon strips on medium-low heat in a covered skillet with a bit of water. The bacon will defrost in just a few minutes. You can turn up the heat to crisp it a little more, if you would like.

SALMON

Salmon is extremely simple to batch-cook in your oven. Cook 3 to 5 pounds (1.5–2.4 kg) of fillets (boneless salmon). Salmon is usually available fresh, and it is best cooked thawed when you are cooking larger quantities. I prefer mine with the skin on. After it is cooked, I often remove the skin, crisp it in a skillet, and add it to my salads. With large pieces of salmon, I slice them into approximately 6-ounce (180-g) portions for baking.

COOK IT IN THE OVEN

1. **Preheat.** Preheat your oven to 450°F (230°C).
2. **Season.** Season the salmon with Old Bay Seasoning, about a teaspoon per pound (5 ml per ½ kg), or a dusting across the fillets.
3. **Skin down.** Place on a baking sheet, skin side down if your salmon has skin.
4. **Bake.** Bake for 12 to 15 minutes, until the salmon is cooked through. It will flake with a fork when it is done. (When white goo comes out of the side of the fillets, it is overcooked.)
5. **Cool.** Allow the salmon to cool before freezing.
6. **Freeze.**

FREEZING METHOD

Place salmon into baggies in amounts appropriate for your salads. Zip the baggies closed, label, flatten, and stack in the freezer.

SALMON
inspiration

SALMON WITH GREEN GODDESS DRESSING, FROM WEEK 5

With a rich protein such as salmon and the creamy richness of the Green Goddess Dressing, I like to keep the toppings on this salad on the light side, adding fresh and crisp bell pepper, red onion, cucumber, and tomato on top of spring mix lettuce. This salad is higher in carbohydrates (34 grams net) because of both the spring mix (12 grams net) and the vegetables. Personally, I do not count carbohydrates from lettuce, but for a lower carbohydrate option, cut out two of the vegetable toppings. Cutting out any two will get you to about 22 net grams of carbohydrates, close to the popular goal of 20 grams for which many people shoot. You could also use a zero-carbohydrate vinaigrette to save just over 3 grams of carbohydrates in the salad dressing. As written, it is about 1,050 calories.

INGREDIENTS
- 8 cups (2 liters) spring mix lettuce
- 6 ounces (180 g) salmon
- 3 mini bell peppers, sliced
- 1 small red onion, sliced
- ½ cucumber, sliced
- 1 medium tomato, sliced
- 1 serving of Green Goddess Dressing

EGG
inspiration

EGG SALAD WITH POPPYSEED DRESSING, FROM WEEK 1

This is one of my go-to travel salads because it is highly portable, simple, and delicious. You can take the boiled eggs with you or turn them into an egg salad at home and transport it. In any case, turn the boiled eggs into a quick little egg salad by mashing them up and adding a bit of mayonnaise and Greek yogurt. I often toss a bit of mustard in as well. I include red onion among the ingredients below, but I show a jar of pickled onions in the photo just to point out this delicious variation. I actually travel quite often with pickled onions because they are already sliced, they include apple cider vinegar should I need it, and they are simply delicious. This salad contains about 1,200 calories and 21 net grams of carbohydrates (6 net grams from the romaine).

INGREDIENTS

- 2 hearts of romaine, chopped
- ½ avocado, sliced
- ½ red onion, sliced
- 1 medium tomato, sliced
- 3 boiled eggs, plus 1 tablespoon (15 ml) mayonnaise, 2 tablespoons (30 ml) Greek yogurt, 1 tablespoon (15 ml) mustard
- 1 serving of Poppyseed Dressing

DEFROSTING METHOD

As needed, grab a baggie from the freezer for your salad. Put the contents of the baggie into a skillet on medium-low heat with a bit of water. Cover and heat until defrosted and warm (about 10 minutes).

BOILED EGGS

Boiled eggs are extremely simple to make and keep around. I recommend always having at least a few on hand to add to your salads when you are extra hungry or when your protein options are otherwise limited. Use either the stovetop method or the pressure cooker method. Both are very simple.

COOK THEM ON THE STOVETOP

1. **In a saucepan.** Place your eggs in the bottom of a saucepan, so that there is room for each egg. I use a deep skillet when I am cooking a dozen or so.
2. **Add water.** Cover the eggs with cold tap water, about an inch (2.5 cm) above the layer of eggs.
3. **Cook.** Cook on the stovetop, bringing the water to a rapid boil.
4. **Cover.** When the water comes to a boil, cover the pan with a lid and turn off the heat.
5. **Continue.** Continue to cook the eggs in the latent heat of the hot water. Remove them in 4 to 6 minutes if you like them soft-boiled. Let them sit for 10 to 12 minutes for hard-boiled. Set your timer for the amount of time you need.
6. **Cool.** As your eggs sit and continue to cook, fill a bowl with cold water. (Use ice water for best results.) When the timer goes off, use tongs to remove the eggs from the cooking pan and submerge them in the cold water to stop the cooking.
7. **Store.** Eat a couple of eggs today on your Ridiculously Big Salad if you need them. Store the remaining eggs in their shells in the refrigerator for a couple of weeks.

COOK THEM IN THE PRESSURE COOKER

1. **Add water.** Add 1 cup (240 ml) of water to your pressure cooker.

2. **Trivet.** Place a trivet in the pressure cooker, and place 6 to 12 eggs on the trivet.

3. **Seal.** Close and seal the pressure cooker. Check the vent to make sure it is set to "seal."

4. **Cook.** Set on manual using these guidelines: 3 minutes for soft-boiled eggs; 6 to 7 minutes for hard-boiled (4 to 5 minutes for in between).

5. **Release.** As your eggs cook in the pressure cooker, fill a bowl with cold water. (Use ice water for best results.) When the timer goes off, use the manual option to release the steam and to stop the cooking.

6. **Remove.** Use tongs to remove the eggs from the pot and submerge them in the cold water to cool them.

7. **Store.** Eat a couple of eggs today on your Ridiculously Big Salad if you need them. Store the remaining eggs in their shells in the refrigerator for a couple of weeks.

SHRIMP AND SCALLOPS

Keep scallops and precooked shrimp in your freezer for extremely quick and easy protein to add to your salads. Prepare each as you need it, in quantities you will finish on your salad that day.

FROZEN COOKED SHRIMP

1. **Thaw.** To defrost, place frozen shrimp in a large bowl of cold water. If you are in a hurry, swish the shrimp around, change the water, and swish again. Swish a few times until it is finally defrosted. If you have a half hour or so, the shrimp will likely defrost without much help.

2. **Skillet.** Warm a skillet on medium heat. Add a bit of butter.

3. **Warm.** Warm the shrimp in the buttered skillet. Remember that it is already cooked. You just need to warm it.

SHRIMP
inspiration

SHRIMP WITH CILANTRO DRESSING, FROM WEEK 3

This salad is another one that's on the lighter side, containing only 900 calories and 21 net grams of carbohydrates (6 net grams from the romaine). You can certainly add some calories and richness to this recipe with nuts, avocado, or blue cheese, to complement the huge flavor of the Cilantro Dressing. You can also load on the shrimp. An entire pound of shrimp (½ kg) is only about 250 calories and 4 grams of carbohydrates.

INGREDIENTS

- 2 hearts of romaine, chopped
- 6 ounces (180 g) shrimp
- 3 mini bell peppers, sliced
- ½ red onion, sliced
- ½ cucumber, sliced
- Cilantro for garnish
- 1 serving of Cilantro Dressing

FROZEN SCALLOPS

1. **Thaw.** To defrost, place frozen scallops into a large bowl of cold water. If you are in a hurry, as with the shrimp, swish the scallops around, change the water, and swish again. Swish a few times until it is finally defrosted.
2. **Skillet.** Warm a skillet on medium heat. Add a bit of butter.
3. **Cook.** Follow the instructions on your scallops for cook time. The cook time will depend on the size of the scallops.

SALAMI
inspiration

ITALIAN SALAMI SALAD WITH KALAMATA OLIVES AND PEPPERONCINI

This salad was left out of the "Six Weeks of Salads" salad tasting, and so you will certainly need to squeeze it in, perhaps when one of the other combinations is not appealing. This salad is so loaded with flavor that you may still be tasting it next month. It combines Italian salami with kalamata olives and pepperoncini, balanced by mozzarella cheese. Topped with Italian Dressing and packed with fresh basil, this salad is a great combination of flavors and nutrients not offered in the other salads featured in this book. This recipe totals about 1,200 calories and 18 net grams of carbohydrates (6 net grams from the romaine).

INGREDIENTS
- 2 hearts of romaine, chopped
- 12 slices of Italian salami, cut into strips
- 4 ounces (120 g) mozzarella, diced
- 4 pepperoncini, sliced
- 10 kalamata olives, pitted
- ¼ cup (60 ml) fresh basil, chopped
- ½ small red onion, thinly sliced
- 1 medium tomato, cubed
- 1 serving of Italian Dressing

GRAB-AND-GO MEAT OPTIONS

We all need some quick options when we find ourselves simply unprepared or miles from home. These are the items I typically grab, but there are surely hundreds of others.

CANNED TUNA

I often use 5-ounce (150-g) cans of tuna and will typically eat the better part of two cans in my salads. I add a bit of mayonnaise and Greek yogurt to the tuna to turn it into a tuna salad.

CANNED SARDINES

Laugh if you will, but sardines are loaded with nutrition, and I think they are pretty tasty. The more cash you have to spend, the less fishy they tend to taste as well. I typically buy them in extra-virgin olive oil and use that oil in the salad dressing. Depending on the quality of the sardines and my feeling at the moment, I add a bit of mayonnaise to the sardines, much like you do with tuna.

SALAMI

This one is great for travel because it comes in convenient slices and is available in any grocery store.

DELI MEAT

I keep deli meat in my refrigerator for kids' sandwiches, and it does come in handy for myself, on occasion. With deli meat around, a Cobb Salad is pretty much always possible.

ROTISSERIE CHICKEN

This is also available pretty much everywhere. Pick the meat off the whole chicken and add to salads, at home or on the road.

All those many months, my subconscious was creating salad dressings that *fit a framework*. In fact, the whole salad had a framework, and the framework was *critical to my success*.

chapter six

Ingredient Guide

As you build your shopping lists in the next section, I offer you here a bit of additional information on the common ingredients you will be purchasing.

COMMON GREENS

Iceberg lettuce. Iceberg lettuce is the nutritionally poor cousin of all the others, and, for that good reason, it is often looked down upon in nutrition circles. However, it has a powerful crunch, and its flavor is mild, if not nonexistent. It is the only lettuce some people will eat. If you are one of those people, you will win eating a Ridiculously Big Salad of iceberg lettuce. I eat iceberg lettuce myself, often in a taco salad. *Preparation*: The lettuce comes in a round head. Simply cut out the core and cut up the lettuce or just rip it up with your hands.

Romaine. The leaves of romaine are long — a head of romaine is not round like iceberg, but rather elongated. You can buy a head of romaine that has all of its leaves on it, or you can buy romaine hearts, which are the slightly crispier centers of the romaine head. You can often buy romaine hearts in packs of three. I often do so and split the three hearts across two salads. However, I have been known to eat a salad with two romaine hearts and have been hearing that many of our Eat Like a Bear! group members do so, too. *Preparation*: Cut off the root end of the head and tear up (or slice) the leaves for your salad. Romaine hearts are my go-to greens for car travel because they are fairly good keepers. I can easily tear them up with my hands, into my big bowl, right out of the back of my car.

Green cabbage. Cabbage is highly filling and has a very mild flavor. It comes in a round head and needs to be cored and sliced, making it an item best prepared in your own kitchen. When I eat it on the road, I typically chop it up in advance. Or you can let someone else chop it for you and buy the bags. I often make a coleslaw when I am having a larger entrée that I do not want to eat on top of a salad. I might eat meatloaf or steak as an entrée but still want all of the filling satisfaction of a Ridiculously Big Salad. I usually turn to cabbage and the coleslaw in these instances. My primary reason is that I simply love the tart/sweet flavor of coleslaw. *Preparation*: Cut out the core and slice the cabbage in half. Taking each half at a time, place the cut side down on a cutting board and make about three slices right through the top and then slice off slivers of cabbage.

Red leaf lettuce, green leaf lettuce, butter lettuce. These are all fairly common lettuces in larger grocery stores with fairly mild flavor. Try them to add variety to your meals. *Preparation*: Prepare them much as you do romaine: Cut out the stems or core and then slice or tear up the leaves.

Kale. Typically, you can find kale in pieces, ready to eat, or you can find larger leaves. If the leaves are larger, simply tear them up to make them smaller. Some people will work oil through their kale leaves to improve the flavor.

Spring mix. Spring mix is a common commercial name used for a package of salad leaves that often includes a combination of romaine, green and red leaf lettuces, and spinach, all often younger leaves. Spring mix is a great convenience product with more nutrient density than just the romaine. The packages tend to keep well if they remain sealed, but they will start to degrade after you open them. This is a good product that will keep in your refrigerator for some days if you do not need to open it immediately.

Chinese cabbage. This is a great option for variety and is especially choice with Asian-inspired dressings and protein toppers. It is a good keeper in your refrigerator, to boot. *Preparation*: Cut off the stems or core and then thinly slice the leaves. If it is a very large head, and you plan to eat half, you can remove the leaves that you will be eating. Make an organized pile on your cutting board, slice them once longways down the middle, and thinly slice your pieces.

Broccoli slaw (and other emerging "slaws"). Companies are finding that if they shred up the previously-not-highly-marketable pieces of things like broccoli stems, we will happily buy them as convenience health foods. I do like this line of salad bases and look forward to trying them all. You will find these items in better-stocked grocery stores, although they sometimes are packaged with dressing and other salad add-ins. Personally, I prefer the packages that contain only the vegetables. The dressings do not meet my standards, and I likely would not pay for them even if they did. Homemade dressings are just so easy to make.

Everything else. There is a whole world of greens out there. Go to your farmers' market or forage in a nearby forest. Some of my best salads have come from wild miners' lettuce growing in my yard.

SALAD DRESSING FOUNDATION INGREDIENTS

Extra-virgin olive oil (EVOO). Costco's EVOO is of good quality for a bargain price, but if you have access to some gourmet EVOO, I would sure go with that.

Mild-tasting salad oil. My choice in this category is avocado oil from a better-known company. The cheap bottles at the dollar store could very well be any oil at all. Those companies do not tend to keep an eye on their supply chain.

Light olive oil would be an option, too, but a problem that both the light olive oil and avocado oil industries face is fraud: Companies make more money filling up the bottle with a cheaper oil and selling it as light olive oil (or avocado oil). In the light olive oil category, there is really no good way for we consumers to know if it is actually olive oil. Fraud is rampant, and the big question, of course, is: If it is not olive oil, what is in the bottle? I do roll the dice on this sometimes and buy light olive oil in bulk at Costco. Actually, truth be told, my husband buys it, and I then use it.

The better brands in the avocado oil industry tend to monitor their supply chain a little better than others. You will notice that Chosen is starting to sell guacamole because, as a company, it is connected to actual, specific avocado trees, not just to a middleman supplier. To me that is at least a signal that we can have a bit more confidence in what is in the bottle. (If I seem ever-skeptical, it is because I *am* ever-skeptical about label claims.)

Mayonnaise. Manufacturers put a lot of strange things into mayonnaise, a product that ought to be just oil and egg. Check the carb content on the label and buy a low one. Aside from the carbs, ideally you will have a good oil in that mayonnaise. I prefer an avocado oil mayonnaise from a better company like Chosen or Primal Kitchen. However, many people in the Eat Like a Bear! group do not like avocado oil mayonnaise.

Personally, I also like the flavor of Trader Joe's mayonnaise, though it contains canola oil, an oil that is controversial in the health world. (I'm skeptical that the canola oil haters are correct, and so I roll the dice and consume it in this mayonnaise. We will see what history says about this issue.)

Also controversial is soybean oil, the main ingredient in many mayonnaise brands on the market, including Duke's, a favorite in the Eat Like a Bear! group. The jury is out on this oil, too. I would eat some mayonnaise from it and not worry about it, but if I am rolling the dice on oil (because we do not really have data on the long-term health effects of some of these oils), I do go in the canola/Trader Joe's direction.

Plain Greek yogurt (or sour cream or ricotta). Greek yogurt is my go-to as the dairy component of a salad. Its flavor is a bit milder than sour cream or ricotta. A plain yogurt (not Greek) works well, too. The biggest issue with buying it is to check the carb content. Start with the yogurt with the lowest carb content in your market and see if you like it in the dressings. If you do, you've found your yogurt.

Apple cider vinegar. A number of companies sell apple cider vinegar "with the mother." "The mother" is just the culture they use in making the vinegar. It is the sediment in the bottom of the jar that is actually healthy. Find an apple cider vinegar with the mother and swish it to get some of that sediment into your salads. Definitely do not buy one of those one-gallon sizes in a plastic bottle from a warehouse store.

Other vinegars. Although apple cider vinegar is the only one I use in this book, you can use other vinegars in the recipes here, including your homemade concoctions. Just be mindful of the carb amount. Some vinegar products have a surprising amount of carbohydrates.

Soy sauce, tamari sauce, or liquid aminos. Each of these items gives you a soy sauce flavor, though some people prefer the Japanese fermented tamari sauce and others the liquid aminos.

Dill pickles. Find your favorites, but check the carbohydrates. There is a surprising amount of sugar in some pickles.

Peanut powder. Peanut powder or peanut flour is a handy ingredient to have around, but check for carbohydrates. This product does have some carbs, but try to find one without added sugar. You can use a regular peanut butter in salad dressings as well, but I like the convenience of the powder and the reduced calories. The reduced calories come from defatting the peanut butter, but peanut oil is not prized for its properties, so I like to get my fat in the rest of the salad dressing. If you go the regular peanut butter route, check for carbohydrates.

Cheese crisps. The Caesar Salad in this book calls for this item. This really is just cheese, toasted in little crunchy nuggets that you can sprinkle onto your salad like croutons. Find them near salad items in the grocery store or bake some in your own oven. (Recipes for "homemade parmesan cheese crisps" will do.)

Broccoli slaw. This is just a broccoli item you can find in many grocery stores near the bags of pre-shredded cabbage or spring leaf lettuce mixes. It is produced by some of the bigger vegetable companies and is simply the ends and pieces of broccoli conveniently shredded for us. Eat Like a Bear! group members suggested mixing it with cabbage to reduce the heaviness of the salad and also to stretch one bag a little further, to avoid smaller-quantity leftovers.

Anchovy paste. Two of the dressing recipes call for this and, I promise you, the dressings do not taste fishy. You can find the paste near the actual anchovies (which are near the sardines, which are near the tuna).

Sweetener (stevia, monk fruit). My go-to sweetener is stevia. It is an extract from an herb, one I actually grow in my garden. Monk fruit is an actual fruit, about the size of a small orange. Both are natural sweeteners that may not affect our blood sugar. Artificial sweeteners like aspartame are controversial, and research shows that they affect our blood sugar even though they are calorie-free. However, in general, the research on sweeteners is only emerging, and we really do not know for sure where we are headed. If I roll the dice on this one, I am heading in the direction of a natural sweetener and just crossing my fingers that we do not learn something sinister about them in the future. That would be a sad day.

I buy a stevia powder and a liquid from Trader Joe's. There are many companies and blended products out there, and they all have slightly different flavor profiles.

Herbs and spices. Freshness is king in the world of herbs and spices. If you have ten-year-old spices in your cupboard, you will not get as much flavor out of them as you would from a fresher source. If you are using old herbs and spices, I would let them sit longer in the dressing before eating it, to bring out some of that flavor. You might even use a bit more in the recipe. If you are buying fresh, I would buy in bulk online or at a health food store (the stores that have bulk bins of these things).

Eat the greens that you can *find*,

that you *like*, and that you can *afford*.

ELECTROLYTE DRINKS

One of the barriers to the keto diet is what has commonly been called "the keto flu," which is simply a set of flu-like symptoms that come as your body adapts to a new diet and begins to process electrolytes differently. I did not experience the keto flu in this round of dieting, but I definitely did in the first low-carb diet I followed more than fifteen years ago. The symptoms were pretty intense, lasted a few weeks, and I had no idea what was going on. These days, an electrolyte drink is a pretty simple solution. The flavor of these drinks does not tend to be fabulous, but the flavor is far better than dizziness, nausea, and leg cramps. Several homemade recipes have emerged in the group thanks to both Anna Sul and Jackie Patti.

Anna Sul, a.k.a. "Bear #2," is an avid drinker of homemade electrolyte drinks and prefers a recipe she discovered in yet another Facebook group, the Magnesium Advocacy Group, founded by Morley Robbins.

Anna says, "My family makes double batches for the day in 28-ounce shaker bottles. We drink one throughout the day. My husband usually drinks closer to two a day. I might drink two if I am on an extended fast or stressed out, but usually one is enough. I use a shaker bottle with a mixing ball inside. The ball helps to dissolve the cream of tartar."

Electrolyte Drink with Cream of Tartar

24 ounces (700 ml) water
1½ teaspoon (6 ml) cream of tartar (potassium bitartrate)
½ teaspoon (2 ml) salt
½ teaspoon (2 ml) whole vitamin C powder, or a few squeezes of lemon or lime

Jackie Patti calculated the potassium and sodium in other common products and offers variations based on what might already be in your pantry.

Lite Salt Variation

24 ounces (700 ml) water
½ teaspoon (2 ml) Lite Salt
¼ teaspoon (1 ml) salt

NuSalt Variation

24 ounces (700 ml) water
¼ teaspoon (1 ml) NuSalt
½ teaspoon (2 ml) salt

Baking Soda Variation

24 ounces (700 ml) water
¼ teaspoon (1 ml) potassium bicarbonate, sodium-free baking soda
½ teaspoon (2 ml) salt

chapter seven

Your Six-Week Plan

My intention with this section is to help you get into a groove with your kitchen preparation. Obviously, you can just move all of this stuff around and adjust as you need to. You will find meats on sale and can cook those as you find them, making changes to this plan to fit your budget and lifestyle.

You will start this six-week plan by filling your pantry with the basic sorts of items you will be using regularly. I provide a pantry shopping list for you to do so. Each week, you can use the shopping list for the week to buy perishable items and to replenish the pantry items as necessary.

You will start with nothing in your freezer, but you will slowly work up to having a healthy little freezer stash that you will just keep replenishing, using the same sort of concept I outline here. Plan to spend about an hour or two each week batch-cooking your protein. As you build your stash, you will be able to take some weeks off in the future. You will also learn to turn two hours of work into one. It all just gets easier with practice. As an aside, if you do not eat pork or beef or if you do not like chicken, just include something else in its place. The process I outline below is highly adaptable.

SPECIAL DIET VARIATIONS

Whatever your diet requirements are, it is likely that someone in the Eat Like a Bear! community has already adapted the Ridiculously Big Salad approach in a similar fashion. While there are many foods in these salads that are off-limits on many diets, there really is no single food item that cannot be replaced with something else, save perhaps

GENERAL PANTRY SHOPPING LIST   NOTES

Mayonnaise

Extra-virgin olive oil

Avocado oil or light olive oil

Sesame oil

Apple cider vinegar ("With the mother" on
the label indicates a higher quality vinegar.)

Soy sauce, tamari sauce, or liquid aminos

Dijon mustard

Mustard powder or jarred yellow mustard

Sweetener (e.g., stevia or monk fruit)

Dill pickles

Hot sauce (e.g., Sriracha), optional

Peanut powder or peanut butter

Almonds/almond slivers

Old Bay Seasoning

Dried herbs and spices: basil, chives, dill weed, oregano,
parsley, paprika, thyme, sage, rosemary, garlic powder,
ginger powder

Poppy seeds

Note: Stock your pantry with herbs, spices, and poppy seeds. A regular grocery store is the worst place to buy these items because they are usually quite expensive and old. In California, Smart & Final has good prices on these items. There are also internet catalog shops for bulk herbs and spices.

the lettuce and greens. If you do not eat pork, you can replace the bacon with turkey bacon, or you can skip the salads with bacon altogether. You can skip the salads with shrimp and scallops if you do not eat those items. If you are dairy-free, you can skip the dairy-based dressings or replace the dairy portion with coconut-based yogurt. At least one group member uses cashew-based yogurt. Of course, if you are nut-free, you would skip the cashew-based yogurt and not add nuts to your salads. Luckily, no specific food is really necessary for your success, although it certainly would be difficult to have a salad without greens. In any case, adapt to your heart's content, and make this framework your own.

WEEK 1

You are just getting started, and you have nothing to eat and no stash whatsoever, so you need to start quick and easy and work your way into a stash. This week you will rely on some easier canned and packaged items — canned tuna, boiled eggs, and lunch meat — to get that jump-start.

Week 1 batch-cooking: This week, hard boil 12 eggs and batch-cook your ground beef. Heat the water to hard-boil your eggs. Boil them while you are working on your beef.

Cook the ground beef, following the instructions in the batch-cooking section, for a lightly seasoned ground beef. I would cook at least 4 pounds (2 kg), but you could cook quite a bit more if you have a couple of big skillets. You are going to batch-cook ground beef because that is a no-fail, easy meat to cook, and because its flavor and nutrients are different from the other convenient protein items on the menu this week.

As you cook the ground beef, work on preparing your salad for the day. You will soon have your protein topper ready because today it will be the ground beef you are cooking.

When you have finished cooking your beef, set aside one portion for today's salad, and freeze the rest in zipper freezer baggies in quantities you will eat on your salad. My quantities are typically about ½ pound

WEEK 1 SHOPPING   NOTES

Ground beef, 3–5 pounds (1.4–2.4 kg)

1 dozen eggs

Tuna, 4 cans (about 5-ounces, 140-g, each)

Chicken or turkey lunch meat, enough for two salads

Greens for salads: one head of Napa cabbage
(Chinese cabbage); 2 3-packs of romaine hearts;
2 heads of iceberg lettuce

Quart (liter) of plain Greek yogurt, sour cream, or ricotta cheese

Additional vegetables for salads: cucumber, red onion,
green onion, radishes, avocado, etc.

(240 g) of cooked meat. If the meat is extra-fatty, you might only freeze about 4 or 5 baggies from a 5-pound (2.4-kg) purchase because more of that weight is fat. You will also be eating some today and perhaps sharing some with family. Definitely consider who else is eating when you are building up your freezer stash. It may be time to buy two large skillets.

This is a costly week with a lot of pantry items. All of the lettuce and greens will probably not fit into your refrigerator. The cabbage can sit in a cool place for a few days, as can the romaine. Eat the bulky iceberg lettuce first. Iceberg also keeps less well than the other greens. When the iceberg is gone, use the refrigerator space for the romaine and then for the cabbage.

WEEK 1
featured salad

THE COBB SALAD

The Cobb Salad is the ultimate in convenience salads and is a great way to get started. In this variation, I use common popular toppings to make a simple and highly satisfying salad. The potential for blandness in the deli meat and boiled egg is balanced well by several fresh ingredients and by the Ranch Dressing. The salad totals only 900 calories and 22 net grams of carbohydrates (6 net grams from the romaine). You can cut the carbohydrates to under 20 net grams by eliminating one vegetable topping. You can add more protein by adding another egg or two, at about 150 calories and 0 carbohydrates each.

INGREDIENTS
- 2 hearts of romaine
- 4 ounces (120 g) of deli ham, sliced
- 1 boiled egg, sliced
- ½ avocado, sliced
- ½ cucumber, sliced
- 1 serving of Ranch Dressing

WEEK 1 SALADS

Taco Salad. Make a salad like the one featured in chapter 5, in the ground beef section. Use ground beef on iceberg lettuce with Ranch Dressing. Add onions, avocado, and a bit of tomato, as desired.

Tuna Salad. Use a romaine heart base with the Classic Vinaigrette Dressing. Add canned tuna with mayonnaise and a boiled egg, sliced or mixed into the tuna. Add optional onions, tomato, avocado, or cucumbers to your salad, as desired.

Cobb Salad. A Cobb Salad is like a deli platter of sliced meats and eggs with lettuce, a featured recipe in this section. Use an iceberg lettuce base with Ranch Dressing. Add sliced chicken or turkey (lunch meat) with two boiled eggs along with sliced cucumbers, onion, avocado, or bell pepper, as desired.

Asian Beef Salad. This salad is similar to that featured in chapter 5, which uses roast pork. You can use ground beef instead, with a cabbage base (Chinese/Napa cabbage if you can find it, iceberg lettuce if you do not like it). Top with Asian Teriyaki Vinaigrette Dressing. Add onion, bell pepper, and other vegetables, as desired. (If you are using a large head of Napa cabbage, you can use half of it next week.)

"Honey" Mustard Chicken Salad. Start with a romaine base and add "Honey" Mustard Dressing. Top the greens with chicken or turkey lunch meat. Add tomato, onion, avocado, cucumber, or bell pepper, as desired.

Poppy Seed Egg Salad. Make a salad like that featured in chapter 5 in the boiled egg section. Use romaine hearts or iceberg with Poppy Seed Dressing. Add three boiled eggs as protein, turned into a quick egg salad. Add sliced cucumbers, onion, avocado, or bell pepper, as desired.

Tuna Salad with Dijon Vinaigrette. Create a romaine base with a Dijon Vinaigrette. Add canned tuna with mayonnaise and a boiled egg, sliced or mixed into the tuna. Add optional onions, tomato, avocado, or cucumbers to your salad.

WEEK 2

You have ground beef in the freezer from last week. This week you will add **chicken** and **bacon**. Boil six eggs if you are out or low. You are cooking the chicken in a very basic way, allowing yourself to use it in a variety of ways over the coming weeks. You will season it only lightly.

Ideally, you will cook the **chicken** in a pressure cooker and just get it over with quickly. If you do not have a pressure cooker, you can bake the chicken in the oven. I would cook a minimum of 3 pounds (1.4 kg) of

WEEK 2 SHOPPING	NOTES
Chicken breasts, frozen, 3–5 pounds (1.4–2.4 kg)	
Bacon, 2 pounds (1 kg), turkey bacon optional	
Tuna, 2 cans (about 5-ounces, 140-g, each)	
Romaine hearts (3-pack); 1 iceberg, 2 dark greens; broccoli slaw *Note: If you like darker greens, and have access to them,* *by all means use them instead of the romaine and iceberg.*	
Medium tomato	
Anchovy paste	
Cheese crisps, optional for the Chicken Caesar Salad (Save some for next week.)	
2 Lemons	
Your choice of vegetables for salads: onion, cucumber, mushrooms, radishes, avocado, a bit of tomato, and bell pepper	
Check your mayonnaise and plain yogurt stash. You will use them for dressings for five big salads.	

WEEK 2
featured salad

ASIAN PEANUT CHICKEN ON NAPA CABBAGE

This simple salad is surprisingly delicious and likely a salad type many people have not tried before. It is already a favorite among a number of group members. I use Napa cabbage, but you could also use regular green cabbage or any of the lettuces. The flavor of the salad dressing stands up well against even the darker greens. In the keto diet world, peanuts are off limits in some circles. If that is you, I am sorry that you will miss this one. I would simply find a different salad because this one does center around the peanut flavor. This salad weighs in at under 1,200 calories and 21 net grams of carbohydrates, including 11 net grams from the Napa cabbage.

INGREDIENTS

- 8 cups (2 liters) chopped Napa cabbage (Chinese cabbage)
- 6 ounces (180 g) chicken strips
- 3 green onions, sliced
- ½ cup (120 ml) peanuts
- 1 serving of Asian Peanut Dressing

chicken. In a smaller pressure cooker, you will probably hit your space limit at just over 3 pounds, so you could be pushing it.

I suggest that you cook the **bacon** in the oven. Most ovens will hold two baking sheets and about a pound (480 g) of bacon. Cook a couple of pounds if you have time to monitor it. Ideally, you are eating about a quarter of it and freezing the rest, but I do know the reality of cooked bacon on a kitchen island: It will disappear in minutes. Freeze what you can. Perhaps buy cooked bacon bits for some of these salads if your bacon keeps disappearing.

As you divide your cooked meats into freezer portions, set aside one portion of chicken to eat today, one portion for later in the week, and two portions of bacon for this week.

You are eating a Chicken Caesar Salad today, so begin that preparation as you cook the meats. You will have to use a blender or food processor to make the dressing, but since your kitchen is already a mess, this is a good day to do it. Make a double batch of the dressing and store the remainder for one more salad next week.

WEEK 2 SALADS

Chicken Caesar Salad. Model this salad after the featured salad in chapter 5, in the chicken section. Use a romaine heart base with chicken and Caesar Dressing. Add optional onions, avocado, and a bit of tomato, as desired. Instead of the traditional croutons, use cheese crisps or toasted almonds. For your chicken, slice the breast into strips and brown in the skillet in butter for a bit of extra flavor.

Broccoli Slaw with Bacon. Enjoy a Broccoli Slaw with the Coleslaw Dressing, like the featured salad in Week 6. Add a bacon topper and boiled egg for extra protein, especially if your family has eaten most of your bacon. Add red onion and perhaps roasted almond slivers.

Chicken Salad with Asian Peanut Dressing. This is the featured salad for this week, and it is delicious. Make enough of the Asian Peanut Dressing for two salads, and store half in the refrigerator for next week. For your salad base, use the other half of your Napa cabbage if you have any left. Otherwise, use a green of your choice.

Taco Salad. This salad is featured in chapter 5 in the ground beef section. Use ground beef on romaine or iceberg. Add Ranch Dressing with a bit of hot sauce/Sriracha if you dare. Add optional onions, avocado, and a bit of tomato.

Bacon, Lettuce, and Tomato Salad. This salad is featured in chapter 5 in the bacon section, and it is memorable. Start with an iceberg base and add Ranch Dressing. Use your leftover bacon. Add boiled egg if you need more protein. Add red onion.

Ground Beef with "Honey" Mustard Dressing. Use a green of your choice topped with "Honey" Mustard Dressing and ground beef. Venture into a darker green (e.g., red leaf lettuce) if you have not yet. The stronger flavors of mustard and beef work well with many greens. Add other vegetables of your choice.

Tuna with Classic Vinaigrette. Use a green of your choice. This will be one of the simpler salads you ever make and gives you a chance to taste a homemade, Classic Vinaigrette Dressing if you have not already. Add onion, avocado, and a bit of tomato to this salad.

WEEK 3

You have ground beef and chicken in the freezer. You may even have bacon if you or your family members did not manage to eat it all. This week you will add **ground turkey** and **pork roast**. Boil six eggs if your stash is low. You are cooking each of these in a very basic manner, allowing yourself to use them in a variety of ways over the coming week. You will season them only lightly, following the directions in the batch-cooking section of this book.

Ground turkey (or chicken) is easy to handle and very simple to add to salads. It is also extremely lean, and if you are working hard to reduce the number of calories in your salad, you will gravitate toward these lean meats. I did that in some of my most intensive periods of weight loss, but, in general, I do find myself a little less satisfied with these toppings, probably because they are lean. I do think it is great for you to try them and see how you feel about them. You will cook the turkey (or chicken)

WEEK 3 SHOPPING LIST   NOTES

Pork roast, 3–5 pounds (1.4–2.4 kg)

Ground turkey or chicken, 3–5 pounds (1.4–2.4 kg)

2 servings of spinach/dark greens; romaine hearts
(3-pack); 3 heads of iceberg

Cilantro, 2 bunches

Frozen shrimp or scallops

1 dozen eggs, if you are low

Cheddar cheese, about a 1-pound (½-kg) block

Dill pickle chips or spears

Plain yogurt and mayonnaise, if you are low

Peanuts, optional

Additional vegetables for salads: cucumber, red onion,
green onion, radishes, avocado, a bit of tomato or bell
pepper, etc.

to do just that. You may love it, in which case you have just found a really easy protein topper to keep around.

You will cook the **pork roast** in a pressure cooker, basically like you did last week with the chicken. I would cook a minimum of four pounds (1.8 kg) and, really, as much as your cooking equipment can handle.

As you pack up your cooked meats in freezer portions, set aside one portion of pork to eat today, one portion for later in the week, and one portion of ground turkey or chicken for this week.

WEEK 3
featured salad

THE EVER-POPULAR CHEESEBURGER SALAD

This memorable salad uses the flavors we all grew up with in the Cheeseburger Dressing. The salad includes other key items you would otherwise find on the burger: pickle slices, cheddar cheese, and white onion. Fast-food burgers are typically served with an iceberg lettuce leaf, making iceberg my top pick for the Cheeseburger Salad experience. This salad weighs in at 1,300 calories and 23 net grams of carbohydrates (13 net grams in the lettuce itself).

INGREDIENTS
- 1 head of iceberg lettuce, chopped
- 6 ounces (180 g) ground beef
- 10 pickle slices
- ½ cup (120 ml) grated cheddar cheese
- ½ of a small white onion, thinly sliced
- 1 serving of the Cheeseburger Dressing

You are eating a pork roast salad today with a Cilantro Vinaigrette, so begin that preparation as you cook the meats. You will have to use a blender or food processor to make the dressing, but since your kitchen is already a mess, this is a good day to do it. Make a double batch of the dressing and store the rest for one more salad in the coming weeks.

WEEK 3 SALADS

Pork Roast with Cilantro Vinaigrette. These strong flavors can withstand stronger greens, so this salad is a chance to try a new green you have not yet tried. However, it is great on romaine or iceberg, too. Add onion, avocado, and some tomato. You will make a double batch of the Cilantro Vinaigrette and try it again later this week.

Chicken Caesar Salad. Like with the featured salad in chapter 5, add chicken strips to a bed of romaine along with the Caesar Dressing. I always add onions, although they are completely optional. Instead of traditional croutons, use cheese crisps or almonds for crunch.

Cheeseburger Salad. Featured this week — add ground beef to a bed of iceberg lettuce along with pickle, onion, grated cheddar cheese, and the Cheeseburger Dressing. You will make a double batch of dressing while you are chopping the pickles, and you will eat it again in a few days because that is how good it is.

Asian Salad with Pork Roast. Enjoy the Asian Peanut Dressing on romaine or iceberg lettuce, similar to the flavors of the featured salad in Week 2. I love green onions on this. Add a few peanuts for crunch.

Ground Turkey with Dijon Vinaigrette. Enjoy the ground turkey on romaine with onion, cucumber, avocado, and perhaps a bit of tomato. The Dijon Vinaigrette Dressing adds a simple flavor variation.

Cheeseburger Salad. One more time. You almost have to.

Shrimp or Scallop with Cilantro Vinaigrette. Use your extra Cilantro Vinaigrette on a green of your choice along with the shrimp or scallops. Add onion, cucumber, and perhaps avocado.

WEEK 4

You have chicken, pork roast, ground turkey, and ground beef in the freezer. This week you will cook bacon and steak strips to add to your stash. Boil six eggs if you are running low.

Today you will use your bacon on a fruity bacon salad, a signature salad you may be adding to your list of favorites.

WEEK 4 SALADS

Strawberry Chicken Salad with Bacon. From the featured salad in this section, try the combination of chicken, bacon, berries, and blue cheese (or feta) over spinach. This may become a quick family favorite.

Steak Strips with Blue Cheese Dressing. Featured in chapter 5 in the steak strips section, enjoy this salad on romaine or iceberg. Make a double batch of

WEEK 4 SHOPPING   NOTES

Bacon: 2 pounds (1 kg)

Steak, 3–5 pounds (1.4–2.4 kg)

Blue cheese, 1 cup (240 ml)

Spinach for one salad; Napa cabbage (Chinese cabbage);
enough other lettuce for five salads

Strawberries or other seasonal berries, enough for
1 cup (240 ml), sliced

Feta cheese, 1 package

Tuna, 2 cans (about 5-ounces, 140-g, each)

1 dozen eggs, if you are low

Plain yogurt/mayonnaise, if you are low

1 lemon

Additional vegetables for salads: cucumber, red onion,
green onion, radishes, avocado, a bit of tomato or bell pepper, etc.

Blue Cheese Dressing to enjoy later this week. Use any of your favorite salad toppings: cucumber, onion, or a bit of tomato.

Ground Turkey with Asian Teriyaki Dressing. Hit the Napa cabbage (Chinese cabbage) again if you liked it last time, or go with romaine or iceberg. If your cabbage is huge, save half for your Asian salad next week. Add avocado, tomato, green onion, red onion, or bell pepper.

Tuna with "Honey" Mustard Dressing. It is tuna again, but with a flavor twist in the "Honey" Mustard Dressing. Use romaine, iceberg, or spring mix plus your go-to vegetables.

WEEK 4
featured salad

STRAWBERRY CHICKEN SALAD WITH BACON

If you have not had this sort of salad before (a combination of meat, berries, and cheese), you are in for a real treat. This salad is likely to get ranked on your list of favorites. On a diet with almost no fruit, the berries in particular provide a delightful freshness. The bacon adds an extra dimension of flavor, but you can consider it optional. I do like Poppy Seed Dressing on this salad, but as you venture out, I highly recommend a variation with "Honey" Mustard Dressing. This salad contains 1,300 calories and 16 net grams of carbohydrates (2 net grams from the baby spinach).

INGREDIENTS

- 8 cups (2 liters) packed baby spinach
- 6 ounces (180 g) chicken breast, sliced
- 2 strips bacon
- 1 cup (240 ml) thinly sliced strawberries (or other seasonal berries)
- ½ small red onion
- 3 ounces (90 g) blue cheese (or feta), cubed or crumbled
- 1 serving of Poppy Seed Dressing

Pork with Blue Cheese Dressing. Use the rest of that Blue Cheese Dressing on romaine or iceberg. This is just like your salad from a few days ago, with a different meat flavor. All of your favorite salad vegetables will go with this one.

Chicken or Shrimp Cobb with Bacon. Make a double batch of Ranch Dressing since you will have some tomorrow. Layer your favorite Cobb ingredients: tomato, cucumber, avocado, bell pepper, and red onion.

Steak Strips with Spicy Ranch Dressing. To your leftover Ranch Dressing add a hot sauce, like Sriracha, to taste to liven up your salad a bit. Use the Spicy Ranch Dressing over a base of greens with the steak strips. Add onion, avocado, and perhaps tomato.

WEEK 5

You have pork roast, ground turkey, ground beef, and steak strips in the freezer. Cook salmon and more chicken breasts (if you are running low on chicken). Boil six eggs if you are low. In my kitchen, I would cook the salmon in the oven and the chicken in the pressure cooker. If you need to use the oven for both, you will have a stretch of time tied up and will want to keep a kitchen timer handy as you work on other projects.

You will eat salmon today and save a portion for later in the week. Freeze the rest in baggies in salad-size portions. Set aside a portion of chicken as well, and add the rest to your freezer stash.

As you cook your meats, you can also begin to prepare the Green Goddess Dressing that you get to try this week. There are so many variations of this one out there. If you do not care for this one, it is still a great framework to come back to and play around with. The herbs in this recipe tend to go well with salmon and pork, so it is a good time to try this combination.

WEEK 5 SALADS

Salmon with Green Goddess Dressing. Featured in chapter 5 in the salmon section, this salad lets you enjoy your salmon over a bed of lettuce

WEEK 5
featured salad

SALMON WITH TARTAR SAUCE

I will admit that the sole reason this salad may be featured here is that I simply love tartar sauce and salmon (or white fish). Maybe it is all about vacations on the coast when I was young, sitting on the dock of a bay and dipping fish into tartar sauce. It just hits the right spot. This salad is a very simple one that highlights the dill pickle flavor characteristic of a good tartar sauce. I add cheese crisps as an option to get a bit of crunch, but some days I really like to keep the flavors simple and centered on the tartar sauce itself. This recipe comes in on the lean end, with 850 calories and 21 grams of carbohydrates (12 net grams from the spring mix). Add more salmon if you feel the need for more protein. A quarter pound of salmon (115 g) has about 300 calories and no carbohydrates.

INGREDIENTS

- 8 cups (2 liters) baby spinach
- 6 ounces (180 g) salmon
- ½ red onion, thinly sliced
- 1 medium tomato, sliced
- Optional: Cheese crisps
- 1 serving of Tartar Sauce Dressing

— one of the darker lettuce greens or a lighter green like romaine or iceberg. Add your favorite vegetables.

Ground Turkey with Asian Peanut Dressing. It is hard to beat this basic and flavorful combination. Use the lettuce of your choice. Cabbage works, too, but I have a slight preference for lettuce, in this case. Add green onions, avocado, tomato, and cucumber.

Shrimp or Scallops with Italian Dressing. This is a very basic, flavorful salad. Choose your favorite lettuce, dark or light. Use a simple Italian Dressing, with shrimp heated or scallops cooked in a bit of butter. Add other vegetables, as you wish. Make a double batch of dressing for later.

Tuna with Poppy Seed Dressing. It is another tuna salad day, with the ever-popular Poppy Seed Dressing. Go for spinach and add your favorite vegetables. Cheese works well on this one, too.

WEEK 5 SHOPPING	NOTES
Salmon fillets (boneless), 3–5 pounds (1.4–2.4 kg)	
Chicken breasts, frozen, 3–5 pounds (1.4–2.4 kg), if you are low	
Greens of choice, possibly 3 servings of spinach or dark greens; 1 head of iceberg; romaine hearts (3-pack)	
Fresh parsley, chives, tarragon, and garlic	
Tuna, 2 cans (about 5-ounces, 140-g, each)	
Plain yogurt and mayonnaise, if you are low	
1 lemon	
Additional vegetables for salads: cucumber, red onion, green onion, radishes, avocado, tomato, bell pepper, etc.	

Pork Roast with Green Goddess Dressing. Have the rest of the Green Goddess Dressing with pork over your favorite green. Add avocado, tomato, cucumber, onion, or bell pepper.

Salmon with Tartar Sauce Dressing. The featured salad this week uses the salmon you baked a few days ago. But whip up the flavor of a seaside café with the Tartar Sauce Dressing. Add the vegetables of your choice.

Chicken Strips with Italian Dressing. Keep it simple today with leftover Italian Dressing, chicken from your stash, and the greens of your choice. Add cucumber, tomato, avocado, onion, or bell pepper.

WEEK 6

You have pork roast, ground turkey, ground beef, steak strips, salmon, and chicken in the freezer. Cook roast beef and more bacon if you are low. Boil six eggs if you are running low.

At the end of the week, you will adapt the Cilantro Vinaigrette to another herb. Choose any herb you want to try. If you have no idea, try a regular garden sage. You can usually find it fresh in larger grocery stores.

WEEK 6 SALADS

Roast Beef on Coleslaw. Use the Coleslaw Dressing. Add hot sauce for extra fire. Add red or green onion. Avocado and a bit of tomato go well.

Salmon with Poppy Seed Dressing. This one is a great, ever-popular combination that never seems to get old. It tastes great on all of the lettuces. Take the flavors in the direction of the featured salad from Week 4, with a bit of fruit and cheese, or go with your standby favorite salad vegetables.

Chicken or Shrimp Cobb with Ranch Dressing. Keep it simple today. Over a bed of romaine or iceberg, add chicken or shrimp, bacon, and your favorite vegetables.

Broccoli Slaw with Bacon. You have had this one before, and it is the featured salad this week. It is packaged broccoli slaw with a Coleslaw Dressing and bacon. Add red onion. Add boiled egg for extra protein and minimal calories.

Roast Beef with Dijon Vinaigrette. Try this one on a dark leaf lettuce like red leaf lettuce or spinach. The strong flavors of the meat and the Dijon Vinaigrette go well with the dark greens. Add vegetables.

Shrimp or Scallops with Asian Teriyaki Vinaigrette. Keep this one simple but try it on cabbage. Green onions are especially good.

Chicken Strips with Sage (or other herb) Dressing. Using the Cilantro Dressing recipe, adapt it to an herb of your choice, and use a dark leaf lettuce. If you do not know of an herb, go for regular sage. It pairs well with chicken (or beef or pork). Add vegetables.

WEEK 6 SHOPPING   NOTES

Beef roast, 3–5 pounds (1.4–2.4 kg)

Bacon, 2 pounds (1 kg)

3 servings of dark lettuce or spinach; 1 large head of cabbage; 1 head of iceberg

Broccoli slaw

Shrimp or scallops, if you are out

Find a fresh herb for your final dressing: fresh sage, oregano, parsley, etc.

Plain yogurt and mayonnaise, if you are low

Additional vegetables for salads: cucumber, red onion, green onion, radishes, avocado, a bit of tomato or bell pepper, etc.

WEEK 6
featured salad

BROCCOLI SLAW WITH BACON

This very simple salad makes regular rounds at my table. The texture of the slaw itself is different from other salads, and you just cannot beat the bacon flavor that plays well against the sweet and tangy Coleslaw Dressing. I use a packaged broccoli slaw product that is increasingly common in grocery stores. It is shredded broccoli. There are other slaw products available that you can substitute here. A basic cabbage slaw is available everywhere, but there are also products that combine broccoli and other emerging additions like Brussels sprouts. This recipe is a good way to try such products. I add egg for some additional protein. As I mentioned with the Bacon, Lettuce, and Tomato Salad, when I have bacon as the protein center on a salad, I tend to add egg. Bacon is high in calories for the protein content. Eggs are low. Considering how good they taste together, they pair well on a salad.

You can also mix and match the slaw products, especially if you are serving multiple people. If my husband and I are both eating, I might use one package of broccoli slaw combined with fine-shredded green cabbage.

This salad measures about 1,150 calories and 16 net grams of carbohydrates (12 net grams from the broccoli slaw).

INGREDIENTS

- 12 ounces (360 g) broccoli slaw
- ½ red onion, sliced
- 4 slices bacon, crumbled
- 1 boiled egg, sliced
- 1 serving of Coleslaw Dressing

An Eat Like a Bear! community member popped one of my salads into the app "Carb Manager," and the salad received a grade of F. Apparently, I *flunked my way* right out of bariatric surgery.

Conclusion

Due to a confluence of unlikely events, I have managed to implement an approach to eating and a discipline that changed my life and, in turn, changed the lives of *many other people*. On most days I am still trying to figure out what I did to come to this point of success. As I see more and more people implement my approach, I find it interesting how some people are completely transformed inside and out by it, while others just use it as a tool to lose weight whenever they might need it.

On the day that I wrap up this book, I feel strongly that the food focus of the Ridiculously Big Salad was a necessary condition for my success, but that it was probably not sufficient. Add to the Ridiculously Big Salad a psychology of discipline and habit, and we likely have the necessary *and* sufficient conditions for weight loss and maintenance. I have had elements of both all these decades, but with missing pieces here and there causing all those years of struggle.

My husband and I are great examples to compare. He jumps in here and there and loses some weight with this method. He goes back to snacking on chips and gains back some weight until he decides to lose it again. He only ever has about 30 pounds (14 kg) to lose and has no apparent health consequences from that weight; as a result, he has no big motivation to maintain his weight loss. I expect he will follow this practice for the rest of his life. In fact, he most certainly will unless he decides to do things differently.

On the other hand, I have lost far more weight and I have actually maintained my weight loss for nearly two years, against all odds according to the medical literature. I discuss the power of habit in the prologue and the personal transformation that comes with the long grind of the diet, but these life-changing benefits come primarily to the community members who keep their noses to the grindstone through holidays, family reunions, illnesses, business travel, and all of the many other situations and events that get us off track so easily. That is exactly what I did out of desperation, and it is something my husband cannot imagine doing. Grind your way through all of those challenges, every day for a year, and see what person emerges on the other side.

Dieting programs always seem to have an "out" when it comes to discipline: the concept of "cheat days" is a particularly popular one. I discourage these strongly. Cheat days may work for people who easily eat a bunch of junk with no apparent physical or health consequences, who can then go right back to being strict. Perhaps people in my husband's category will just have "cheat seasons" losing and gaining the same 30 pounds. In our community, far too many people struggle to keep their cheat day from turning into a cheat week, and they end up in a constant cycle of falling off the wagon and struggling to get back on. If you fit into this category, think about the habit you are creating with your cheat day and your future struggle with the wagon.

In my opinion, if you are going to focus your energy on weight loss, go big, and just get it done, for as long as it takes.

Vacation cruise? Hammer, hammer, hammer.

Potluck dinner? Hammer, hammer, hammer.

Holiday party? Hammer, hammer, hammer.

There are almost always some healthy options at these events. You can also eat a bit before just to be sure. You can abstain from eating entirely. The choice is yours to make beforehand.

If you need a break, hone your maintenance skills for a bit, as I discuss in the chapter on discipline. Maintenance mode definitely takes less energy, but it does keep your head in the game, and it is, in fact, a habit you probably *do* want to embrace, one that will serve you for the rest of your life. Take some days or weeks to hone your maintenance skills, get comfortable in that maintenance routine, and then jump back in like a beast to lose another 20 pounds (9 kg). Rinse and repeat as necessary.

Create a structure that works for you, but be mindful that as you do the hard work of losing the weight, you are training yourself for *something*. Let that *something* be a tool you can use for the rest of your life.

As for the tool, allow me one last story about a wedding I attended just a few weeks ago. It was the first wedding I have attended since I started all of this. In these many months, people have asked me: "What about the *wedding cake*? Should I eat it?" While it might be easier to walk away from the cake at a fundraiser, walking away from a wedding cake is a whole other level of strictness. In fact, weddings are such important events that it begs the question: *Should* we forego the wedding cake? I had opinions on this question all of these months, but I had simply never tested them.

First, I remember my mind-set in August 2017, as I was gearing up for extreme strictness. I was grieving my future without the food and drink I knew I simply had to give up. With my avid interest in herbs and foraging, I was making the best cocktail mixers you can imagine and enjoying them every single night with bourbon. The cocktails were so good and unusual that I probably could have made real money selling the mixers at Southern California farmers' markets. They satisfied my cravings for flavor, sweetness, and alcohol, and they gave me a great sense of satisfaction in general because of how clever they were, created right here from herbs on my property and from the forest. To make matters worse, my mom started fermenting wine from wild berries and other local fruit, and they started coming of age right as I started this diet. In my world, these drinks were very hard to walk away from. Sure, I also felt a small tinge of pain at the thought of not having the occasional cake and muffin, but these were nothing compared to the cocktails and wine. I was grieving giving them up and also pretty concerned that on a bad day I would relapse and fall off the wagon.

In any case, I did go through grieving as I started this diet, not having a clear view of my future in terms of the weight loss and in terms of remaining compliant. It did all feel like a punishment, and the mourning was deep, but I wanted to walk more than I wanted to drink, and so I was willing to give it a go. I just did not have a clear view of the other side and where the path would take me. I certainly expected a lifelong struggle with that cocktail because that is simply how much satisfaction it brought me. It may have been the high risk of a relapse with the cocktails that caused me to be extra-strict and diligent as I got started.

All of those feelings were deep in the "me" of 2017. If you read the prologue, you have some idea of how the "new me" feels about alcohol. Sure, I would love to live in a world where I could drink the cocktails without consequence, but that is not this world, and I simply value the life I have now far more than the momentary pleasure I get from an oregano cocktail or wild blackberry wine.

Now that I have found a combination that works for me, how I evaluate my choice is simply completely different from how it used to be. I describe it in the prologue as the choice sets: "fat or fatter?" and "trim or fat?"

For my whole life I evaluated the cocktail from the "fat or fatter?" choice set. I could abstain and be fat or I could drink and be fatter. The consequence of being "fatter" when you are already "fat" is minimal. Sure, the creep of the scale is powerful, but every single choice to drink is almost rational. With a choice set of "trim or fat?" I find myself in the highly unexpected position of teetotaler. If I can be trim, for the first time ever, I simply evaluate the cocktail in a whole new way.

As for the wedding, I made my decision the night before: I would eat at the wedding dinner, watching the carbohydrates and unconcerned about the calories. I would also allow myself the champagne and the cake. That is the rule I made for myself the night before, the most lenient rule I have made for any one day to date since I started. Even though I have been completely strict about alcohol, I do feel the champagne toast is an important part of the event and that the "clank" of the glasses and the "sip" is important to me. I toasted and I took a sip. It is a fabulous ritual. I passed the rest of my champagne to a friend without remorse because I simply did not value the experience of drinking, weighed against my choice of "trim or fat?" I certainly realize that one glass will not make me fat, but boundaries have kept me trim, and alcohol is not a boundary I am willing to cross.

The wedding cake was a homemade carrot cake, a bit of a tradition in this social circle, complete with homemade butter cream frosting and rum-soaked raisins. I might report how it tasted, had I eaten any. I had given myself permission to do so, but I simply did not value the experience of eating the carrot cake more than staying thin, given my new choice set.

Practiced over many months, completely diligent and strict, I forged a new set of habits that made it possible for me to have this choice set for the first time in my life: "trim or fat?" Constantly foregoing the drinks and the desserts all those months so that I could lose the weight forged a whole new way of thinking and behavior. That new habit served me well at the wedding dinner, and it is mine to keep if I choose to cultivate it.

Consider the alternative cheat day approach: What would be the habit I would have forged all those months if I had allowed a cheat day monthly or even weekly? Certainly, after the weight loss, I would have eaten the cake at the wedding, at the potlucks, at the business meetings, during holiday parties, and so on. I expect I would face the coming holiday seasons wondering, "Is this the moment it all falls apart?" Worse, it very well could be that moment. The world has an awful lot of potlucks.

My newly married friend and husband then visited my home two weeks after their wedding for dinner, complete with handcrafted wine and homemade brownies with ice cream. I am not sure anyone noticed my alcohol abstinence, but when those brownies got served, a number of necks turned right in my direction, wondering, I expect, "Is she going to eat one? How can she not eat one?" I did not even consider eating one and felt no mourning whatsoever over the situation. My mind-set was simply completely different from that of all of the others at the table. I do not need to be like my friends, and they do not need to be like me. They eat the brownies. I choose not to eat the brownies.

I do have the sense that some people feel sorry for me in my strictness or think I have gone completely overboard in my austerity, embracing some sort of cultish asceticism. From my perspective, here on the other side, I do actually enjoy my food far more than I ever have, and so that reputation of asceticism always strikes me as odd. In addition, my eating restrictions are inconsequential when weighed against the many other things in life I am actually able to do. It is difficult to communicate how completely life-changing it is to lose half your body weight and just be able to walk, *easily*.

All of that said, I have good days and bad days. On bad days, I am highly mindful of that human urge to eat, to soothe the wounds. However, an interesting thing happened in this regard, too: With a year of requiring myself to be ultra-strict, I found comfort in activities such as walking and swimming to get through those bad days. Now in maintenance, on a bad day I can fully immerse myself in a swimming pool or a lake and just swim around, taking it in. It is comforting to me. I seek it out on a bad day. It is a new release I found to comfort myself during that year of the long grind. In the world where I had simply fallen off the wagon, I would have never found this new tool and, instead, I would be struggling with the wagon.

I am struck by another point in all of this. Over these many decades of struggle, most diet gurus and weight-loss programs have tried to turn me into something I am not: a person of moderation. I do basically everything in my life in the extreme and almost nothing in moderation. A moderate person, trying to be helpful, perhaps a weight-loss coach, might suggest that I drink just one cocktail or just one cocktail a week. Perhaps he would suggest that I allow myself one cheat day a week and drink a cocktail on that day, a completely rational argument for a moderate lifestyle. After decades of failing at being a moderate person, I am completely happy and satisfied embracing my extreme self. I do not have to struggle daily with how many cocktails I am drinking because, in fact, I am drinking zero, and zero is far easier than keeping one cocktail from becoming two. The boundary is simply easier.

In terms of my general approach to food, I happen to manage my eating by putting it in a boundary defined by the clock. Some people find it odd, but I thrive within the structure. The boundary has biological effects in terms of insulin, and so it works like crazy for both my biology and my psychology.

Many important factors come together in all of this, which are driving my success and that of the members of the Eat Like a Bear! community. In a book about salads, it is easy to focus on the food. The food will most definitely help you lose weight, but I expect it is the grind itself that is the life-changing component. Put your head down and grind, mastering the new tools that you need to make this work. Grieve a bit, but do not focus too much on this side of the divide. If you can grind for a year, you will simply be a different person on the other side, with a whole new world of choices available to you.

I look forward to your story.

The Eat Like a Bear! community was born on Facebook, prodded by a *chance encounter* with millennial Instagrammers wandering in a forest, like some sort of 2018 *cultural time capsule*.

The Eat Like a Bear! Origin Story

For decades (and even today), had you asked me my opinion of the weight-loss industry, I would have told you that if you want to wallow in a cesspool of mediocrity, the weight-loss industry would be a great place to do just that. For an industry that peddles products that only half work, taking advantage of people at some of the lowest points in their lives, *mediocrity* is a kind word. The weight-loss industry is one with which I have never wanted to be associated. That said, I am highly aware of the irony of this book and of the weight-loss community I founded on Facebook in July 2018, Eat Like a Bear!

Indeed, starting the Eat Like a Bear! community may be the strangest and most unexpected thing I have ever done. Had I any notion of what was brewing, I would have a slew of "before" pictures, "during" pictures, DEXA scans, blood work, and every other relevant artifact. As it was, I was positioned to have bariatric surgery with no hope or expectations whatsoever that I might end up trimmer than I have ever been, leading a growing community composed primarily of older women.

I founded the group on July 9, 2018, but through the spring and summer of 2018, I was highly focused on another pursuit. As spring of 2018 came, and I was down 100 pounds, I got out and hiked and foraged around my home in California's Giant Sequoia National Monument. With my new energy and focus, I began a YouTube channel on herbs and foraging and was ready to build a digital foraging empire. Clearly, it would be difficult to be more awesome than when you are foraging in the forest around you, and I was ready to do just that. Those initial videos were fairly bad, but I was gearing up to launch a series in the summer, far better produced, with great stories. In the meantime, I had some weight-loss videos on YouTube for friends and family, more for convenience purposes, on a tiny new channel with no subscribers and no plan. More notably, I posted a few videos on Facebook, including a video called "Eat Like a Bear!"

The "Eat Like a Bear!" video responded to an ongoing reaction to my one-meal-a-day diet: "You're starving yourself!" I pointed out that bears purposefully get fat to starve off their fat in hibernation. Not eating for twenty-three hours in a day is not close to record-setting in the animal world, and it certainly is not starving, especially when the one meal has north of 1,000 calories, well above the bariatric model of eating. If what I did was starve myself, I should have starved myself far sooner.

I published the "Eat Like a Bear!" video on May 9, 2018, and continued to build my foraging empire. I got burned out, took off on a big road trip to the Pacific Northwest, and then got refocused on my foraging video goal at the big annual video conference, VidCon. I returned home from VidCon on June 23, ready to launch the new foraging series. I went on hikes and shot some footage in late June and early July. However, I noticed something extraordinary on the morning of July 6 as I was cooking my meal: My satellite internet service had enough speed for a live video for the first time. I quickly jumped on Facebook live with a "What I am eating" video. Two ladies who had seen my videos in the spring reported that they had lost 30 and 40 pounds (14 and 18 kg). One said, "You were my inspiration. Nothing else worked until you!" The other offered, "I was inspired by your journey. I started on May 18th and I've lost 42 lbs [19 kg]." Their comments took me back. Friends and family members were having great success with my approach, but now two people following me on the internet were reporting the same. I was aware that I was having a small impact, but I certainly never intended for it to become my full-time focus. I was busy foraging, after all.

By late afternoon on the same day, I was driving on our rural mountain road and slowed down for four millennial hikers who looked lost and completely out of common sense, walking down the center of the road. I rolled down the window and asked if they needed help. "We are looking for the best sunset view!" We chatted a bit, and I took in their positive, happy-go-lucky energy and offered a variation of my favorite line: "Would you like to see the sun set from a historic brothel?" (Yes, my house was a brothel in the 1920s, and it is a line I shamelessly use for notoriety among the right demographic, and surely hipster millennials fit the bill.)

Amanda Rose and Anna Sul (a.k.a. "Bear #2")

We hung out that Friday evening and then again on Sunday. All the while Friday's live video experience and the two ladies who lost weight swirled in my mind, causing me great angst as I tried to stay focused on my foraging video plan. By Sunday, with my newfound friends, little tidbits had crept into our conversations about video making, including my recent trip to VidCon. I realize now that they must have been perplexed: "Who is this middle-aged woman in this historic brothel in the middle of a forest who just went to VidCon?" What I did not know about them is that they were in the entertainment and video industry, and two had sizable platforms on Instagram. It was a highly unlikely encounter here, in the middle of absolutely nowhere, on July 6, 2018. By noon on Sunday, one asked me directly: "What do you *do*?" I took a breath, felt all of that swirling inside, and blurted out, "I don't know what I am doing with my life!" I explained my weight loss, my foraging-empire-to-be, and my shock over actually providing leadership on the most ridiculous topic of weight loss, shaking my head and ending again with "I just don't know what to do!" Four jaws dropped in unison, and one of the ladies looked directly into my eyes and said with all certainty, "You have to do this!"

The next morning, I went live again on Facebook and announced that I would "create a small Facebook group" so we could stay in touch and support each other. Shelley, profiled earlier, joined on day 1, July 9, 2018, and was our first official member to hit the 100-pound (45-kg) loss mark, about nine months later. About 1,000 people joined in the first week, mainly via my Facebook page, and the group continued to grow to about 7,000 by September, mainly due to some food-related videos I posted on Facebook, highly recognizable as foraging-like diet food. We got a great crew of people interested in weight loss and also projects like infused vinegar, pickled eggs, and stinging nettle soup.

However, as I became more mindful that we had a burgeoning community, I also became dissatisfied with the message of infusing chocolate with lavender or making elderberry cream cups because, quite frankly, as awesome as those projects are, no one trying to lose more than 100 pounds (45 kg) should be eating dessert at all. (Sorry.) I also knew people could learn to infuse herbs into their desserts anywhere, and if I was going to give up my foraging empire to join the weight-loss community, the least mediocre way to do that would be to attract some of the most significant weight-loss cases out there and see some serious transformations. That surely would not be difficult since I would simply need to attract myself, as a start.

My mind was focused on this topic in August 2018 while on a cross-country road trip with my sons, relocating a hand-me-down Ford Explorer the long way from Pennsylvania through Michigan, the Dakotas, and Wyoming. We stopped in Yellowstone National Park, where we had been one year before on a vacation to observe the total solar eclipse. We re-created some of our photos from the previous year. Most notably, my teenager and I stood at the 45th parallel sign north of Yellowstone, each of us reaching our hand to the other, touching from either side of the 45th parallel, in perfect tourist fashion, as if that sign were planted on an exact geographic line. In a photo now seen by more than half a million people, the photo credit belongs to my then nine-year-old son Alastair, who took a series of photos, some of which even included all of our body parts. Of the many photos young Alastair took, some did match well the photo from the year before. We jumped back into the car and hit some other Yellowstone landmarks, with about three days ahead of us to get home.

While I was fairly diligent with Instagram up to that moment, when I saw the new set of photos, I was completely speechless. My mind pondered the photos on those three days of driving and, in particular, the message I hoped would attract people to our community. I returned home, pensive and pondering. I vacuumed for about a week, wearing out the carpet, and shot a video now called "A Postcard from Yellowstone."

The community grew from 7,000 in the fall of 2018 to 20,000 in February 2019, largely due to the Yellowstone video, a video that would come to shape the culture and success rate of our community in a way that I would not appreciate for a year. The new group members included Maria, also profiled earlier, who found us on January 4, 2019. The subsequent growth has come from friends and family referrals, with a focus on women over fifty, women who have always struggled with their weight, who have a whole lot of weight to lose.

Although our community is based online, we have a core of members in my home region, California's Central Valley. My county, Tulare County, is California's capital of obesity and diabetes. Many community members come from Tulare County and neighboring Kern and Fresno Counties. Known as California's most productive agricultural region, nearly half of our children and more than one-third of our adults struggle with obesity. In my background as a food forager, I look for remedies on the trail — a plantain leaf to counteract the itch of an insect bite or a lamb's quarters leaf to alleviate the sting of a nettle leaf — the problems and solutions all found side-by-side in the forest, if you know where to look. California's most obese counties are bordered on the north, south, and west by the nation's most prolific agricultural land for the production of salad greens, a remedy waiting here for us in Central California, one that we have always known is important, but a remedy missing a few pieces. It is my hope that as this community grows, members can take this simple and accessible solution and fashion it to fit their own needs and lifestyle.

The stories emerging from the community are extraordinary, and they make me proud, but I do spend a lot of my time feeling very emotional. So much of what I do every day requires me to think back on what it felt like to weigh 280 pounds (127 kg), and it is a memory I would simply never revisit if I were not in this position. I see the emotions swirling in the community as well, at all stages of the transformation, but especially at the life-changing stages where we simultaneously celebrate and have our minds completely blown. I suspect that, for a variety of complex reasons, we have one of the most highly engaged communities on the internet, with people focused on the biggest grind of their lives and then those staying to help others achieve the same success.

Much like I surprise myself almost daily with the new physical experience of being half my size, I am taken aback more so with the online community that we have forged and the daily success stories that fuel us. The community is obsessed with bears, rooted in the intermittent fasting portion of what we do, but perhaps a mythical bird emerging from the ashes of a fiery pit might have been an appropriate symbol, had any of us — the early adopters — any sense of what lay ahead.

The Eat Like a Bear! community was born on Facebook, prodded by a chance encounter with millennial Instagrammers wandering in a forest, like some sort of 2018 cultural time capsule. It has been fueled by viral success cases emerging from the early adopters in the community, including many from California's obesity capital, leveraging a tool — flexible, inexpensive, and simple — that grows right out of the earth nearby.

No surgery, no drugs, no branded products.

Required: Your own bootstraps (and perhaps a lot of salad greens).

You don't need drugs, surgery, or branded products. You don't even need hope. I had none and *my life changed* anyway.

– Amanda Rose, "Half My Size" video, February 2019

EAT LIKE A BEAR! DIGITAL COURSES

EatLikeaBear.com

The Eat Like a Bear! website offers a growing number of digital courses.

The "Cooked RBS" digital course includes recipes and extremely simple cooking methods for the "Cooked Ridiculously Big Salad." These recipes use the popular framework of The Ridiculously Big Salad, but the dishes are cooked rather than being raw salads.

The Eat Like a Bear! Jump Start has been a popular module to get people started. It uses the highly-reviewed forthcoming book *Eat Like a Bear! Jumpstart: The Three-Day Challenge Unpacked.*

The Eat Like a Bear! Psychology Module is the newest offering on the website and currently is a video-based series on the mindset of success by Amanda Rose, in which she leverages research in social science utility theory, applying it to food choice and addiction.

Check out the Eat Like a Bear community in Facebook for subgroups such as Silver Bears (people 65 or more years old), Ursa Major (starting weights over 300 pounds [136 kg]), Shake Like a Bear (exercise), Bear Threads (fashion), Bariatric Bears (bariatric surgery), BearFat Burners (extended fasting), and more.

Find Amanda Rose on Facebook, Instagram, YouTube, and Pinterest.

About the Author

Amanda Rose, Ph.D. is a "half my size" case, down to 140 pounds from 280, trimmer than ever, below her high school graduation weight. She promotes a highly replicable, inexpensive, and healthy approach to weight loss that has caught fire among an older demographic with similar lifelong weight struggles, embodied in the meal type she calls the Ridiculously Big Salad. Her approach combines the popular frameworks of intermittent fasting and ketogenic eating, in a fashion that is both highly effective and simple to implement.

With a Ph.D. in political science and a minor in statistics, Amanda has worked as an analyst for government agencies and has been an active member of the natural foods community for two decades. She is a strong advocate of consumer information and choice and has given a TEDx talk on the complexity of free choice in consumer decisions.

Amanda lives with her husband, Sander, and sons, Frederick and Alastair, in the Giant Sequoia National Monument, on private land in California's Tulare County. Known for its record-setting Giant Sequoia trees, Tulare County also holds California's record for high rates of obesity and diabetes. With emerging viral Eat Like a Bear! success cases in Tulare and neighboring Kern, Kings, and Fresno Counties, locals call this geographic center *The Belly of the Bear*.